Like A Tree Cut Back

Like A Tree Cut Back

Part History · Part Memoir · Part Meditation

Michael McCarthy

smith|doorstop

the poetry business

Published by The Poetry Business
Campo House,
54 Campo Lane,
Sheffield S1 2EG
www.poetrybusiness.co.uk

The publishers are grateful for the encouragement and support of Carlow College.

Designed & typeset by The Poetry Business.
Cover Image: *The Orchard* by Donagh Carey (www.donaghcarey.com)
British Library Cataloguing-in-Publication Data.
A catalogue record for this book is available
from the British Library.

Smith|Doorstop is a member of Inpress
www.inpressbooks.co.uk.
Distributed by NBN International, 1 Deltic Avenue,
Rooksley, Milton Keynes MK13 8LD.

ISBN 978-1-912196-36-4
eBook ISBN 978-1-912196-49-4

The Poetry Business gratefully acknowledges the support
of Arts Council England.

Supported using public funding by
ARTS COUNCIL
ENGLAND

With thanks to

Dr Tom Mc Grath
and
Fr Conn Ó Maoldhomhnaigh

Contents

Part Three – A Chink of Light

Part Four – A Tree Cut Back

Part Five – My Journey of Conversion

PREFACE

*L*ike *A Tree Cut Back* combines two biographies in one: it interweaves the life of Michael McCarthy and the history of Carlow College, St Patrick's, in Ireland. The College motto, *rescissa vegetior assurgit* – 'that which is cut back burgeons forth more abundantly' – encapsulates essential features of both.

The book opens with 'The Accident' that cut short the young life of Michael's brother, James, leaving an indelible mark on the lives of his family members. Overshadowing Michael's early years in 1950s Ireland, it is also the tragedy that renders sweeter and all the more delightful the innocent pleasures of rural childhood, a 'Growing up Among Ferns'. James's death remains a backdrop in 'Beyond Childhood', through the triumphs, trials and tomfoolery of Michael's young adulthood and his studies at Carlow College. Later on, after Michael has been ordained a Catholic priest, the childhood trauma continues to make its presence felt, manifesting itself in a sense of inferiority and deep-rooted anxiety offset only by acute powers of perception and an eloquent humour that sets him apart from the rest. In 1990s Chicago, Michael finally turns to confront the unspent grief of the little boy he was. He finds, as he does so, a gift for poetry and new access to the healing power of the written word.

That gift finds full expression in the poems of his four previously published collections, written after the Chicago sojourn, some of which are reproduced here. We are grateful to Bradshaw Books for permission to republish 'The Gift', from *Bird's Nests and Other Poems* (2003); to the *Queen's Quarterly: A Canadian Review*, for 'The Handball Alley' (2018); to Smith|Doorstop Books for 'The Morning Bobby Kennedy Died' and 'Transfiguration' from *At the Races* (2009); and to the same press for 'Monica' and 'In Memoriam' from *The Healing Station* (2015). Michael puts his gift to new form in the autobiographical sections of this book, his first adventures in prose; and it burgeons forth abundantly in the two historical sections relating to Carlow College.

Before meeting his own history backwards, surrendering to the moment and embracing his younger self in 'A Tree Cut Back', Michael reflects on the two-hundred-year history of Carlow College in 'A Chink of Light'. He merges historical materials archived in the College's O'Keefe Library with new poems generated by the encounters and conversations that enriched the period he spent as poet-in-residence at his alma mater in 2017. Mining the biography of one of its first students, Fr John Joseph Therry, he orchestrates a chorus of voices that testify to the horrors of penal colonies in nineteenth-century Australia and Van Diemen's Land. First published in Rev. Eris M. O'Brien's book, *Life and Letters of Archpriest John Joseph Therry, Founder of the Catholic Church in Australia* (1922), Therry's correspondence becomes the raw materials for 'found poems', as Michael calls them, which give voice to convicts and to others who sought, in the hours before death, the 'consolation of Religion'. These poems bear witness, too, to the threat to authority posed by figures like Therry: they show colonial secretaries and governors conspiring against him and his support for the poor and downtrodden. Noteworthy, here, is the alignment not so much of Irish versus English or of Catholic versus Protestant in the penal colony as of powerless versus powerful. Noteworthy, too, is the absence of voices from those positioned even lower down that social scale, the 'Aboriginal youth', represented here only as Therry's prospective charges or as the 'Black Native' that one of the convicts confesses to having murdered. Offering a messier picture than we are perhaps used to seeing in our history books, 'A Chink of Light' brings to life the desperate struggles that pitted the nineteenth-century poor against the ruling classes and their administrators across the colonial globe.

Michael's diagnosis with incurable pancreatic cancer in April 2018 threatened an untimely truncation of *Like A Tree Cut Back*. Fortunately, as he wrote in an unpublished letter to Fr Conn Ó Maoldomhnaigh, he was blessed in his last months of life, not only with 'a calm spirit and a deep gratitude for the life I have been given', but also with 'a burst of creative energy'. He thought of this as the upside to a terminal diagnosis and wished for 'the necessary time and the creative clarity' to 'pull it off'. Michael found the time: he rested his pen on a complete typescript on Friday, 8th July, just three days before he died. The creative clarity left little for those he asked to look after the project – Peter and Ann Sansom, Richard Scholar and me – to do. 'My Journey of Conversion', the last part of the book, offers an eloquent retrospective on the entire process of Michael's turning to poetry and evolving spirituality, as well as on the book.

For the benefit of that PhD student of 2116 imagined in 'In Memoriam', who is studying Michael's work among that of other 'Forgotten Irish Poets', we declare that we did make one change to the order of sections in his final draft. The July 2018 typescript opened with 'A Chink of Light', moving on to the current parts 1, 2, 5 and 4. We feel justified in re-ordering things both by the permission he gave us to 'follow your literary instincts' and by an email he wrote in May 2018 after a sleepless night in hospital. In a burst of that creative energy he had hoped for, he envisaged a new structure for his book: for reasons we hope will be clear, we have reverted to that. All other aspects of the text remain as Michael left them: his extraordinary testament to an ordinary life well lived.

Ita Mac Carthy
Durham and Reenroe, March 2020

Part One
RERAHANAGH
GROWING UP AMONG FERNS

The Accident

It's eleven o'clock on Saturday morning. But I don't know this. The day and time are all the same to me because I'm only four.

Georgie Chambers is ploughing the big field at the cross. There is sudden commotion. My mother is shouting and she's running out of the house. Something is after happening above on the road. My brother Ando is running after my mother. I'm running after my sister Nora. She's heading for the house of our neighbours Danny and Mrs Mahony. I can't keep up with her. Suddenly she's not there.

I'm standing at the bend on the road at the top of the hill, and I can't see where she has gone. What I can see is the way the grass covers the ditch. And the stones coming through the grass. I can see each individual stone clearly. I can see each bit of grass. I wait a long time. There is no sign of my sister. Something has happened, but it must have happened somewhere else.

I'm in the garden in front of the house. I'm looking through the gap in the hedge. I see my father walking slowly. He is carrying my brother James in his arms. Another man, taller than my father, is carrying my brother Tim. Tim is draped over the man's shoulders. The man and my father carry the two of them into the house.

I'm sitting on the settle in the kitchen with my brother Ando. Something is going on below in the parlour. We're not supposed to go down there. People keep coming from the parlour. They come through the kitchen, and out to the back kitchen and out the back door. My mother comes through with my uncle. My uncle has his arm around my mother's shoulder. My mother is crying. Then my uncle goes back into the parlour. He comes out again. This time he has his arm around my father's shoulder, and my father is crying.

My brother is counting people as they go past. Some of them are crying, and some of them are not crying. My mother is crying the most, then my father. My brother says he cried when he saw the cart turned upside down on the road. I didn't cry at all.

My sister Kathleen comes home from school and she is crying. Danny Mahony is there, and Mary Jerry Connie, and the doctor, and the priest. Then my godfather Jerome comes in a motor car. People are taking pillows and a rug to the motor car. Jerome and my father take Tim away in the motor car, and everything is very quiet.

Georgie Chambers and his son are standing near the water tank at the gable end of the house. Georgie Chambers says it is a sad day. The two of them walk away from the house. They are carrying ploughing tackle: a horse's collar and harness. The way they walk is what a sad day looks like.

My cousin Rosemary comes and my mother takes her upstairs. I follow them up. James is lying on the bed. He is not moving. He looks the same as a statue. I ask my mother why he looks like a statue. My mother says it is because he is in heaven. Rosemary starts to cry.

Mary Jerry Connie washes the blood out of the pillowcases. She cleans the house, dusting it and getting it ready for all the people coming. She washes the cups and saucers and the Holy Pictures. She is washing the statue of the Sacred Heart. I tell her: 'Don't tickle him neck.'

There are people and more people coming and coming. The house is full of people. There are many more people outside the house. Some of the people are in the shed where the cart with the broken shaft is. People are looking at the cart with the broken shaft. People are looking at the dents in the milk churns. People are telling each other what happened.

Everybody goes away and all the horse and carts go to the funeral. Mary Jerry Connie minds me and my brother.

Paddy and Liam come, and my father tells them for God's sake to take away the black mare. A man comes to fix the shaft of the cart. He puts steel bands around where it is broken. The churns can't be fixed. The dents will have to stay on them. The pillowcases are clean now, but you can see the marks where all the blood was.

People come to the house and say to my mother and father: 'I'm sorry for your troubles.' Whenever we say the rosary my father says we must pray for Tim in hospital, and poor James in heaven.

I hope Tim is having a nice time in hospital. I hope James is having a nice time in heaven. I think they should come home soon because everybody is lonesome. Everybody cries because they are lonesome. I am lonesome but I do not cry.

When we meet people in town, or after Mass, they come up to my mother and father and talk about poor James. They ask them how Tim is. My mother tells them he is in the Mercy Hospital. He has a fractured skull. The doctor says to be prepared for the worst.

After a long, long time my mother tells us that Tim is coming home from hospital.

My father has gone with Jerome in the motor car to bring him home. Everybody is very excited. When Tim arrives home he comes into the kitchen and everybody is laughing and crying, and fierce excited. I go all shy because I haven't seen him for such a long time. I run and hide in the corner beside the dresser. I cover my face with my hands.

Tim says he has brought me a present but I'll have to come and get it. I won't come because I'm too shy. I peep out from between my fingers. I see that he has Cadbury chocolate bars.

They are wrapped in purple and there is a big pile of them. I keep my face hidden in the corner, but in the end I stretch out my hands behind my back. Tim puts the chocolate bars into my hands and I run upstairs and begin eating them.

When Tim comes up to go to bed I hide my face under the clothes. I peep out now and then. I'm watching him, to see what he looks like. He pretends not to notice. After a while I get braver. And then I'm sitting up in the bed, looking across the room at him in the other bed. He begins talking and asking me questions. I start telling him the news, and about all the things that have been happening while he was in hospital.

Now when we meet people in town and they ask how Tim is doing, my mother and father say 'he is doing fine, thanks be to God'. Then they talk about 'the little boy'. They say they prayed for us. Sometimes they start crying. Sometimes my mother starts crying as well. Sometimes coming home from town in the trap my mother and father talk about poor James. Sometimes my mother starts crying again.

My brother Tim goes back to school. My father tells him to be very careful. He tells him to mind himself. Soon he is himself again. Soon he is riding horses again. My father is pleased to see him riding a horse. Seeing him on a horse frightens my mother.

My father and mother say James was an angel and that was why he went to heaven. Sometimes I wish he hadn't gone to heaven. And sometimes I wish he'd come home.

Sometimes I wonder if I went to heaven would they be lonesome after me like they are after James. They keep saying that James was a good boy. I'm getting tired of everybody being lonesome for James and no one being lonesome for me.

THE BEDROOM

I climb the stairs, lingering as long as I can on each step. I examine the shine on the brass stair rods that I watched my sister polish, the way they neatly tuck into the tarpaulin. On the landing I look out through the back window. I see where the pigeons live in the trees. Beyond the trees, cattle are grazing in the fields that slope all the way down to the river. The summer sky is still a clear blue but I've been told it is past my bedtime.

To the left, three steps up and straight ahead, that's my parents' bedroom. To the right, three steps up and straight ahead, the girls' bedroom. The door on the right, before the girls' bedroom, is the boys' bedroom. That's where I'm heading because I'm a boy.

In our bedroom there are two double beds. My two brothers sleep in the bed at the far end. I share the bed nearest to the door with my uncle. I sleep on the inside, next to the wall. There are blankets and a patchwork quilt on each bed. My brother, one year older, will be sent to bed before too long. My brother, nine years older, won't be coming to bed until much later. My uncle will come later still.

There is a curtain on the window but it is not drawn. I like to see the daylight for as long as I can. There is candle grease on the stone plinth at the bottom of the window. A leftover from the Christmas candle, when every window in Ireland has a candle in it so the Holy Family can find their way to Bethlehem.

The walls are painted yellow. The floor is covered in brown tarpaulin with faded yellow squares on it. A corner has curled up where the leg at the top end of the bed keeps getting pulled across it. There is a hole where the leg at the bottom of the bed has worn through. There are white enamel pots for peeing, with handles on them under each bed. There is a picture of the Sacred Heart on the wall.

The shape of the ceiling over the stairs protrudes between the beds, half dividing the bedroom. It gradually slopes upward and then has two steps at the top which are used as shelves. One has blankets on it. The other has a wooden money box my big brother made. It is painted green and nailed onto the shelf. There's a lock on it but I know where he hides the key. My big brother has also invented an electric light for himself, a used radio battery with a piece of wire coming out of it. The wire is pinned along the groove of the shelf and attached to a bulb from a flash-lamp over the bed. There is a switch half way between the battery and the bulb. We're not allowed to touch it because we'd only wear out the battery. Sometimes we switch it on when he's not there.

Looking up at the white ceiling I trace the lines between the ceiling boards. Here and there I can see spaces between the boards. I try to see through these cracks, but it's no good because it's dark up there and all I see is the shadow of darkness. I wonder about the world up there because sometimes after dark I can hear mice running along the ceiling boards having fun. The sudden patter they make is like the patter of raindrops when it's just starting to rain.

I like looking at the knots on the boards. They are still visible even though the ceiling has been painted many times over. These knots have interesting shapes. One looks like a spinning top. There is a small perfect roundness at its centre. I imagine it spinning, and decide that I'll ask for a real spinning top for Christmas. Another one is the shape of a pear or a kangaroo depending on which way you look at it. Another has no shape at all that I can think of.

When my brother comes to bed we tell each other stories. I wonder out loud what else lives above the ceiling. What my brother is more concerned about are the creatures under the bed. The ones that come out in the middle of the night. He tells me how once he woke up to find his leg had slipped down inside the bed and something had got a hold of his foot. All he knew for certain was that his foot was 'between teeth'.

My mother shouts up the stairs: 'Will ye stop talking and go to sleep.' We don't take much notice. It's hard to sleep on these long summer nights when it isn't even dark yet. Later on, my father shouts: 'Go to sleep this minute.' That quietens us all right. In a while we begin to whisper again until eventually we drift off to sleep. Sometimes we are still awake when my big brother comes up. We watch him as he switches on his electric light to see if it is still working, and then gets into bed. Occasionally we are still awake when my uncle comes up. Sometimes we ask him questions and get him to tell us stories. He tells us the names of stars, and all about the Comet with its long bushy tail. It will be in the sky every night until it disappears, and then it won't come back for another hundred years. My favourite thing in the sky is the Rory Bory Alice because it has such a nice name.

Sometimes gravity rolls me into the hollow in the middle of the bed and my uncle tells me to 'push in out of that'. On one occasion when I'm a little older and he's not in a good mood he says, 'shove in will you. You're taking up half the bed.' I say: 'Let you take up the other half.' I overhear him later telling this story. It makes all the big people laugh. I realise everybody thinks I'm a very funny and clever boy. I like that.

My uncle gets up early to bring the cows in for milking. My big brother gets up a little later and goes out to the stall to milk. Sometimes I hear them and wake up. Sometimes I go back to sleep again. On a Saturday night my uncle shaves. He gets a basin of water, then rolls up his sleeves and stands in front of the shaving mirror. He dips the furry shaving brush into the basin, rubs the shaving stick on it and lathers up his face. Then he goes at it with his cut-throat. You can hear the scrape of the razor on his hairy stubble. He is very careful but sometimes he cuts himself. He puts little pieces of newspaper on his face to stop the bleeding.

When he's finished shaving he spends a long time polishing his strong black shoes until he is entirely satisfied with the shine. On Sunday morning he gets up early for going to Mass. All he has to do is put on his shirt and tie and his blue suit, and then his socks and shoes. Sometimes he finds a hole in a sock and says: 'Well blasht it for a story.' The last thing he does is put on his bicycle clips, then he's out the door and gone. We won't see him again until dark night.

I'm supposed to be asleep while all this is going on, but the noise wakes me and I find it all very interesting. Once, I interviewed him.

'Where are you going?'
'I'm going to Mass.'
'What are you doing?'
'I'm putting on the style.'
'What style?'
'The style that Mary sat on.'
'And did Mary sit on your style?'

There is a skylight out on the landing. You can see it through a space on the top corner behind the door. There is a similar space into the girls' bedroom. Sometimes you can see their outlines reflected in the glass of the skylight.

When my other uncle the Priest comes to stay, things are rearranged. He sleeps in the girls' room. A curtain is put across the boys' room and the girls sleep in my brothers' bed. My two brothers come in with me, and my uncle goes out to the hay shed. When this happens we have to be very quiet because my uncle is home from the missions and he finds it very hard to sleep. We can hear him saying his prayers. Sometimes he gets up in the middle of the night and goes out walking because he can't sleep.

He tells us great stories about what China was like, and the different ways they had for torturing people. When he gives a sermon about it during Mass he gets very excited and shouts. All the big people talk about it afterwards and some of the women start crying and the men shake their heads in wonder. They give him money for the missions. He gets lots of letters from the postman and nearly all of them have money in them. My brother says he'll be a priest too when he is big enough, and he'll sit in the parlour all day reading letters and counting money. I want to be a priest too when I grow up because I was called after my uncle, and as well as having the same name we have the same birthday as well. He says I'm very clever and witty because the big people have told him what I said about the style that Mary sat on. I'll be a priest for sure. Being in China is very exciting.

The other thing I remember about the bedroom is the day I got the measles. My big brother was putting up a wire fence and I was holding the bag of nails for him when I began to feel all funny. I could see the wind blowing through the grass like it often did but somehow it was different. It had a sort of yellow colour and it looked very hot. The next thing, I had pains in my legs. Marmalade was the cause of it. I could feel the briars from the marmalade inside in my legs and they were hurting me. I tried to explain to my mother but she just kept asking, 'what marmalade are you talking about, child?' I didn't know what she meant because there was only one marmalade and the briars from it were hurting me inside in my legs. When the doctor came he lifted up my shirt. I was covered all over with spots. He said I had the measles and I'd have to stay in bed until I got better. He said the marmalade in my legs was only growing pains.

The last thing I remember about the bedroom is the day I ate my big brother's sweets. He went to the fair with my father and after they had sold the heifers he bought some sweets for himself. I was busying around the bedroom minding my own business when I accidentally brushed up against his coat. I heard the rustle of the paper bag the sweets were in and I had a look in his pocket to see what sort of sweets they were. They were toffees. The wrapping paper had partly come off one of them and rather than going to all the trouble to wrap it up again I thought the best thing was to eat it. I put the wrapping paper back in the bag so it would take up the same amount of space. Later I went back to make sure everything was alright and I found another sweet that was peeping out of its wrapper. I fixed it the same way as the first one, making sure the bag was still full. Later on again, I went to check that everything was ok and I found another one. I thought it was only fair that my middle brother should have some sweets as well. I wouldn't tell him where they came from because he'd only take some himself and not even make sure the bag was still full.

Later that evening when my big brother came in he went upstairs. He was very cross when he came down. He said: 'Who stole my sweets?' My mother asked him what did he mean and he showed her the bag with all the sweet papers and only a few sweets left. I said I didn't know anything about them, but my middle brother said I gave him sweets. He said he didn't know where I got them. I tried to explain that I was only trying to make the bag tidy and keep his pocket from bulging, but he kept throwing it in my face for a long time saying: 'You stole my sweets.'

THE SYCAMORE TREE

There's this tree around the corner from our house. It is a sycamore tree. It is very leafy, and the leaves have the same number of fingers as I have, only their fingers are much bigger than my fingers. The tree has a fork you can sit up on like a saddle. I'm wondering what it would be like to climb up and sit on it. Is it the same, or different from being on a horse? It's different. The bark is not smooth like a horse but it's exciting. I'm not supposed to be up here and that's part of the excitement. I can hear the birds singing and the wind blowing. Then I take off my trousers and I am just like the birds except I have no feathers. I can feel the bark of the tree against my bare bottom, and the breeze blowing around my bottom, and it is very exciting.

Everything is going grand until my big sister comes around the corner. I try to put my trousers on before she sees me, but it is no good. She says she won't tell anyone, but the way she says it worries me. It's a lot worse than saying she'll tell on me, because she can threaten me with it any time she likes. And how can I be sure she won't tell on me whenever she feels like it.

Then I begin to worry in case she saw me that other time up in the field near Mahony's house. All I was doing that time was finding out what it was like being like the pigs. I went along the ground on my knees to be about the same height as a pig. Then I took off my trousers so I could feel the wind on my bottom the same as the pigs. I liked the wind blowing around my bottom, and I knew the pigs liked it as well.

I didn't like the rooting on the ground though because it was very cold and my nose hurt. The part I liked best was when the wind was blowing around my bare bottom. But I didn't think I was supposed to be doing it. That was all part of the fun of it until my sister saw me up on the tree and said she wouldn't tell.

If any of this ever comes out I don't know what will happen. Maybe the next time they are cutting the bonhams they'll mix me up with them. I can smell the disinfectant already, and the bowl of boiling water. I can see my uncle holding the bonhams on his knees with their back legs held out, and my father dipping the penknife in the boiling water and cutting them. I don't like the way they squeal when he cuts them.

Then the postman comes. He has a parcel for me. When I open it up it is a horse from my aunt in California. My aunt is a nun. It is a lovely bay horse and it has a shine on it. It has a white blaze on its forehead and a flowing mane. It has four white legs but one of them has got broken in the post. I blame the postman. My brother says it's no bother to fix it with glue, and it will be as good as it ever was. Still, I wish the leg wasn't broken. He fixes it all right, but ever after there is a weakness in that leg so that it breaks easily. He might get fed up fixing it.

I overhear my mother talking to Mrs Mahony. They are comparing each other's children. My mother says that when I was small you couldn't keep trousers on me. She said as soon as she'd turn her back she'd find my trousers hanging from the apple tree. My sister must have told on me. My mother shouldn't be telling this to a complete stranger. I run away and hide behind the turf rick. How can I ever go to Mahony's house again? I hope they don't find out about the pigs.

I soon forget all about it though because Jo Mahony is much more fun that anyone in our house. She's younger than me, and I don't know anybody else younger than me anywhere. I go there first thing in the morning and I stay until Mrs Mahony sends me home. And as soon as I get home I want to be off there again but my mother won't let me.

'Don't be bothering Mrs Mahony every minute of the day,' she says. So I sneak off when no one is looking, and where do I go? Mahony's. But I pretend to myself that I am going somewhere else, and it just happens by accident that I end up at Mahony's. I play with Jo for hours and hours. Mrs Mahony disappears for a while, and when she returns my big brother is with her. He says I have to come home.

This puzzles me because, strictly speaking, I'm not at Mahony's at all. I'm somewhere else. So if I'm not here in the first place I can't go back with my brother because I am somewhere else. This however, doesn't seem to work. My brother insists that I must go home at once and when I'm not making any move he says that if I don't go home with him now I'll have to stay forever. Mrs Mahony says: 'Where will he sleep? The only thing I can think of is he'll have to sleep with Jo.' This is very worrying. I've never slept in a stranger's house, never mind sleeping in a stranger's bed. Mrs Mahony and my brother are laughing at me and I don't like it. It's like the time my mother told Mrs Mahony about my trousers.

THE MIRACLE

My father comes home from the creamery. He empties the separated milk from the creamery churns to the old churns where the milk will turn sour and my uncle will feed it to the pigs. You can see the dents in one of the old churns from when James was killed. My father un-tackles the horse, lets him take a drink of water and then puts him out in the field. My father is thirsty after all this and my mother brings him a drink of sour milk from the kitchen. Then she brings a bucket of scalding water and a scrubbing brush and washes the creamery churns so that tomorrow's milk won't go sour. While she is doing this my father tells her all the news and interesting stories from the creamery.

One day it doesn't happen like this. Instead my mother is standing by the hedge waiting for him. He ties the horse to the wall and comes straight over. They have a short conversation, then they both turn and walk towards the house. When they get as far as the pillar my father puts his arm around my mother's shoulder. They hold each other and then they walk towards the front door with their arms around each other. They are both crying. It doesn't look the same as lonesome.

One morning I come down stairs carrying my clothes as usual. I'll warm my bottom in front of the fire, and then my mother will dress me. This morning there is no sign of my mother. And the fire is not lit. When my big sister comes in I ask her, where's Mammy? She doesn't answer me because she's busy. I tell her I'm cold. She says not to be bothering her because she has enough to do. I ask her again, where's Mammy, and she says not to be bothering Mammy either because Mammy is busy. Then she tells me to put my clothes on myself and get out of her way. I have had just about enough of this carry-on, so I head back upstairs. I'm still carrying my clothes. When I open my mother's door there is a strange woman there. She is a big fat woman and she won't let me get past the door. 'You can't come in here,' she says.

How dare she! How dare she tell me what I can and can't do in my own house! I push past her, but she grabs hold of me and bundles me outside the door and closes it in my face and I'm left standing there. It is the coldest feeling I have ever known. After a long time I go back downstairs with my clothes still in my arms and my sister is getting the breakfast ready. I ask her to put my clothes on and she tells me I'm not a baby anymore and I'm big enough now to put my own clothes on.

I don't know how long this misery lasts, but sometime later I'm taken upstairs to see the new baby. Everybody is saying it is 'a mericle'. I don't know what 'a mericle' is but I don't like it much.

Apart from the matter of not being let in to my mother's bedroom the new baby is interesting enough. She is very small. I've never seen anyone that small before. I don't like nurse O'Neill though. She is very bossy. I think she is the cause of all the trouble around here and the sooner she goes the better. The new baby drinks milk out of a bottle. The bottle is the same shape as a banana. The milk has to be warmed first, and the bottle and the nipples have to be put into boiling water.

My big brother is up in the grain loft. He is taking the pram down from the rafters.

He is going to get it all ready for the new baby. When he looks inside he says nothing only: 'Come here and I'll show you.'

When I look in I see a litter of baby mice. They are pink and tiny and have no hair, and they wriggle in their nest like little pink worms. They are about the same size as the baby's toes. They can't put the new baby in with the mice and they can't use the pram after the mice being in it. But my brother takes the pram outside and scrubs it from top to bottom. Later he paints it so it will look nice, and oils the wheels so they won't squeak and wake the baby. I don't think she'd like it much if she knew about the mice, but I'm not going to say a word. I'm really fond of her now, and I'm glad that nurse O'Neill is gone.

The new baby is growing quick. She drinks milk, and sleeps, and sometimes she cries.

It's a very thin kind of a cry, not like ordinary crying at all. Her hair starts to grow and it is almost pure white. Nobody has hair as nice as hers. I don't lift her up because I might let her fall, but sometimes when she is in the pram I help push it. The pram looks very nice and she looks nice in the pram. I'm getting very fond of her, and I'm never ever going to tell her about the mice.

Today is a church holiday. We've been to Mass as usual and afterwards we've gone shopping. Now we're standing at the side of the street by the Maid of Erin. My big sister is there and my big brother, and my middle brother, and my mother and the baby. There is a big bus parked at the side of the street. My mother gets into the bus with the baby and we all wave at her. She is going to my grandmother's house for a bit of a rest.

The next thing I see is my middle brother going into the bus. When I go to follow him into the bus my big sister pulls me away from the door. She says: 'Come on away and we'll go for ice cream.' I'm in favour of ice cream any time, but right now I have to be on that bus with my mother. I escape from my sister's grip and I run to the door of the bus but the man blocks my way. That's when the hullabaloo starts in earnest. I wail at my very loudest but it does me no good. The man won't let me on the bus. My sister is trying to coax me away, but I know what the plot is and I am determined not to be got the better of. Now my sister has me in her arms and she won't let go of me and the bus starts to move. I can see my middle brother inside the window with a smirk on his face. I hate that smirk. It's because he's going and I'm not. I'm determined to hate him for as long as I live.

I continue to wail after the bus has gone. I know it is a waste of time and the battle is lost but I do it anyway. Eventually my big sister persuades me to come to the snack bar for an ice cream cone. It is a big soft cone with a twirl at the top. My sister says: 'Now so, isn't that the fine ice cream.' I just lick at it and say nothing. I wouldn't give her the satisfaction.

I don't know how long they stay away, but when they come back my brother wants to tell me all about it. About Uncle Stephen, and the twins, and the sheep, and the big mountain, and another thing, and another thing. I don't want to hear anything about it, but I don't want to miss anything either. So I pretend not to be listening, but I'm taking it all in and trying to make the pictures in my head. My baby sister has grown while they have been away. And her hair is longer and whiter, and she is the best thing that ever happened around here.

GOING TO MASS

Every Sunday and Holy day we go to Mass in the horse and trap. I'm ready in my new suit, so I watch my big brother harnessing the horse. First he puts on the winkers and then the collar and hames, the one with the bells on it. Then he throws the saddle over the horse's back and ties the belly band tight. The tackle goes around the horse's backside, and my brother pulls his tail through the crupper that hangs at the back. The horse enjoys all this. He likes going to Mass. My brother backs the horse into the trap, then lowers the shafts and fits them into the loops on the harness. My sister fixes the cushions on the seats. They are made of leather and wool and stuffed with horse hair. My mother brings the rug and says: 'Hurry on or we'll be late.' She's wearing a long brown coat and a hat with a bow that has a net over it. My big brother sits on the same side as my father. My other brother and I sit on my mother's side. My father and mother sit at the back of the trap. When my father gets onto the step, the trap heaves back because he's heavy. He's wearing his second best hat. He keeps the best one for funerals. My sisters sometimes go to Mass on bicycles because the trap is getting too small for all of us to fit. When we're all in my father takes the reins, cracks the whip and we're off.

The wheels make a nice rubbery noise, but the road is a bumpy road until we get as far as the cross. The main road has wheel tracks at the sides and is rutted along the middle from the horse's hooves. We reach the real main road just after Holland's Cross. From there on the road is tarred. On our way to Mass we pass other people in horses and traps or bicycles because we have a fast horse. My father likes fast horses. If a motor car comes my father pulls in to let it pass. You can always tell if we're late, because the crows are on the road picking at the fresh dung. They only begin doing that after everyone has gone to Mass.

My father lets us out at the bottom of the convent hill. He goes up the hill and ties the horse to the wall near the gate to the Brothers. Inside at Mass the church is full. We get a seat near the back and I'm sitting next to my sister. The seats are a light-coloured shiny wood. The confession box behind us has the priest's name on it. The priest starts saying Mass and all the people say their prayers. Most of them have rosary beads. I'm wearing my new suit. It's a bit like rosary beads because I can follow the stitches on it, especially around the label that has the name of the tailors who made it. The next thing my sister is cross with me. She's hissing at me and telling me to stop that and say my prayers. I think she's cross because I have a new suit. I'm sure if my mother saw her she would tell her to let me alone.

There's a man going around with a plate taking the collection. He looks very serious. He has a shirt with the collar turned up at the corners instead of down. The two points of the collar stick up next to his chin. He looks around with his eyes without moving his head. There must be something wrong with his neck.

There are some old women wearing black cloaks with a hood over their heads. There's fancy stitching around the edges all the way down to the ground and back up the other side, and around the hood like more rosary beads. My mother says there's no need to be frightened of them, but that only makes it worse. It's like being frightened by a horse's head looking out

21

over a ditch on a dark night.

There are two women that look like each other, and one of them has an iron at the bottom of her shoe. It looks like a stirrup. There must be something wrong with her leg.

My mother says I shouldn't be looking at people like that because it's bad manners.

There is a boy who always wears a cap that covers the side of his head. He only takes the cap off when he goes into Mass. His hair is combed down over his ear. There must be something wrong with it. Maybe he has no ear, or maybe something happened to it. Maybe a rat ate it one night while he was asleep? I wouldn't like it if a rat ate my ear. I'm glad my uncle and my two brothers sleep in the same room as me. It makes it harder for a rat to steal in during the night and eat your ear. You'd think you'd wake up if a rat tried to do that to your ear. Maybe he'd do it so quick that he'd be gone before you could even wake up. Then you'd wake up and the pillow would be all sticky with your blood, and your ear would be gone. And then you'd have to wear a cap or else have your hair combed down over your ear, and everybody would notice it in Mass instead of saying their prayers. If a rat ate one of your toes that wouldn't be as bad because you could cover it up with your shoes and stockings and people wouldn't notice.

After Mass we bless ourselves in the holy water font. My sister tells my mother I wasn't saying my prayers. She says all I was doing was admiring my new suit. My father stays outside the church after Mass talking to people his own age. Every week he talks to a man called Naylus. They knew each other long ago. They were comrades during the troubles. On Holy Days they go for a drink and the rest of us go shopping. We don't do that on Sundays because the shops are not open on Sundays. I don't like shopping because my mother never knows what she wants. She says we'll take a look first. She looks at things and asks what price they are, and then she doesn't buy them. Sometimes she buys things for me and I like that, but she won't buy anything for me today because I have a new suit.

After shopping my mother goes in to Nagles' Pub. Mrs Nagle fills a big stone jar with porter to take home. Sometimes

Mrs Nagle brings us into her kitchen and gives me biscuits. I like biscuits. Sometimes while we are waiting for my father to finish talking we go in the snug, and my mother has a glass of sherry and I get a glass of lemonade. I like lemonade. I like the fizz of it. Afterwards we all go back to the horse and trap with the messages my mother is after buying. The horse is ready for going home. My father puts the trap back on the horse and we all get in and go home and have our dinner.

CHRISTMAS

It's the day before Christmas. The first thing to do is the goose. Yesterday my mother killed the goose. You have to have strong hands to kill a goose because a goose has a very strong neck. Next you have to pluck the goose straight away because it is easier to pull the feathers out while the goose is still warm. I help my mother to pull some of the feathers. Today she will make a fire with papers and some sticks outside the back door to burn the down that is left on the goose after the feathers are all plucked. Next she'll cut off the wings and make them into quills for sweeping the table and the window sills. Then she'll cut off its feet and I'll play with them, to find out what it feels like to be able to paddle. My mother will put stuffing in the goose's belly and when it is cooked we will have stuffing as well as goose.

Now I watch my sister cut turnips in half. This is so she can turn them into stands for the Christmas candles. After she cuts them in half she carves out a hole in the round side of the turnip the same size as a candle. When they are ready I take one to every window in the house, upstairs and downstairs, and one for the back window. That makes seven altogether.

While all this is going on the postman comes. His name is Jack Reagan and he gets a drink in every house for Christmas. It is very late, almost dark when he gets to our house. He stumbles in the door and says, 'God blast that for a trastle, it nearly knocked me.' There is no trestle at the door in our house. My father says it's because he is lighting with whiskey. He gets a glass of whiskey in our house too. He says: 'Good luck and a happy Christmas,' and puts the whiskey back on himself and swallows it down with one big swallow. Then he gives a loud noise as if the whiskey is burning his throat. When he leaves our house his legs are staggery and he can't ride his bike. So he walks up the road and he props himself up with the bike.

When it is dark night we light the candles, and then we go out to the field behind the house and we see the candles in all the other houses for miles around. The houses seem much farther away when they are lit up at night than when you see them in the daytime. Mickey Ireland's house has only two candles because it is a cottage and there are only two windows, one downstairs and one upstairs. We look at the stars as well. They are the candles in the windows of heaven. Heaven has a lot of windows.

When we go back inside we have lemonade and Christmas cake. My sister has made a Christmas cake with green icing on it. She gets the bread knife to cut a slice for each of us, but when she sticks the knife into the cake it collapses in a heap. Someone has been turning the cake upside down and eating it from the inside. My sister is very cross. She blames my big brother. She says she knows it was him because he doesn't like icing. My brother says why would he do a thing like that, but his face has gone red. My sister says that Christmas is spoiled and she'll never bake another Christmas cake as long as she lives. But she calms down after a while and divides what's left of the cake between us all, except my brother. Then she gives him some as well, because it's Christmas. I won't be hearing any more about the sweets I accidentally took out of his pocket that time after he went to the fair.

My mother says we have to go to bed next because Santy wouldn't come to a house until small people were gone asleep. I wrote a letter to Santy and posted it myself. My mother asked me to tell her what I asked for, and I told her some of the things but I didn't tell her all of the things because if you ask Santy for too many things you might not get anything at all and I didn't want my mother to think I was asking for too many things.

My mother wakes us very early on Christmas morning because we are going to go to first Mass. She lights the candles because it is pitch black. The first thing I hear is my brother shouting: 'He came. He came.' Santy has brought us some of the things we asked for. He has brought me a green hat with a feather on it, and a ball, and a bugle, and some balloons, and a car. He has brought my brother a lorry. His lorry is bigger than my car. My mother says it's because he is bigger than me and Santy takes notice of things like that. Maybe he'll bring me a lorry next year!

My mother says hurry on and get ready because Timmy the Hens will be here in a minute to take us to Mass in his big car. His real name is Timmy Hennessey. When we get to Mass there is a crib that looks like a cave in the rocks. Jesus is in it with Mary and Joseph and some cattle and sheep and a donkey. There is a choir singing high up in the gallery. They're singing 'Hark! The Herald Angels Sing'. The angel with the nicest voice is called Nancy Donovan. At the end of Mass the priest says three Hail Mary's for the conversion of Russia, and a happy and a holy Christmas to everyone. My mother brings us to pray to baby Jesus in the crib.

It is just getting light when we get home. My father pays Timmy the Hens ten bob for bringing us to Mass in his big car. We can play properly with our presents now, because the first thing is to go to Mass and after that we can play as long as we like. It's a wonder how Santy managed to come down the chimney without getting soot all over himself, because there is a lot of soot in our chimney. My mother says soot is no bother to Santy. We have great fun playing ludo, and snakes and ladders, and other games and we make a lot of noise. We can smell the goose cooking. My mother says: 'Will ye stop arguing, or Santy will come and take the whole lot of them away.' So we go outside and blow our balloons and play ball for a while.

When we come back in the goose is out of the oven and it smells nice and it's gone all brown. My mother puts the thigh of the goose on my father's plate. That's because the goose's thigh is the right size for a man. My brother gets more goose on his plate than me. My mother says it's because my brother has a bigger belly. She tells me to eat what I have first, and then I can have some more. In the end there is plenty for everyone.

The next day is St Stephen's day and the races are on in Drimoleague. There are always fights the night of the races when people get drunk. Nobody from our house is going to the races this year because Birdie Hayes is dead. My sister says I should be crying for her because she is my godmother. But I'm in a sulk because I'm not being let go to the funeral. I've never been to a funeral because funerals are for big people. But how am I supposed to pray for her if I'm not even let go to the funeral. If anyone has a right to go to this funeral it's me.

It has been snowing heavily but now the sun is shining and it makes everything sparkle and shine. I'm in the field below the house. All the big people are gone to the funeral. We have a new dog. He is a black and white collie. They are trying to teach him not to go rambling off. It's no good tying him up because as soon as he's let loose he's off to God knows where. So they tie a log to his collar so that he will not go too far. When he follows me down the field the log drags in the snow until it becomes a snowball. The farther he follows me the bigger the snowball gets, until he gets stuck in the snow and can't go any further.

When my sister comes home from the funeral and sees him she says: 'Wisha look at the poor dog.' She takes the collar off with the snowball attached, and the dog goes off jumping and yelping. He runs around in the snow and makes it sparkle. My sister asks me why have I a puss on me. She says there is enough tragedy in the world, and that I should be saying my prayers for poor Birdie Hayes instead of going round with a puss on me.

I look down across the slope of the land to the river. The fields are white everywhere. There are cattle in the northern fields and my uncle will have to carry hay to them while the snow lasts. Years later I learn that my godmother Birdie Hayes died in childbirth. That she was laid out in her coffin with her child next to her. But for now, here in this snowed-over meadow with the dog raising haloes in the snow, with the cattle sheltering in the northern fields, and the river meandering along minding its own business, all I know is that there's nobody taking a blind bit of notice of me. I'm left all on my own. And what's the point in your godmother being dead if you're not even let go to the funeral.

School

My teacher is called Miss Sarah. She is also called Mrs Fitzgerald. Our classroom is upstairs. We have to go through Miss Hanna's classroom first to get to ours. Miss Hanna gives me a sweet because we are related, and because I'm a very good boy. Miss Sarah doesn't give me sweets, but when we've done whatever she told us to do, she says: 'That'll do for the present.' She keeps saying that but there's never any sign of a present. I ask my mother when is Miss Sarah going to give us the present she keeps promising us?

Sometimes Miss Sarah gets cross and she screeches at people. She has a ruler in her desk and if a boy or girl is very bold, she makes them hold their hand out and she gives them a slap. She never gives me a slap because I am always a good boy. That's why Miss Hanna gives me sweets. Then one day Miss Sarah lets out a screech at me, and then she makes me hold out my hand and she gives me a slap of the ruler. My hand gets very hot and it's hurting like mad. Then I feel like a very bad boy. Miss Sarah says I was looking out the window at the wide world instead of paying attention to what she was saying.

Sometimes Miss Sarah takes singing lessons. She has a tuning fork. She hits it on the desk and tells us listen to the sound it makes. Then she sings: 'Do,' and gets us all to sing do-re-mi, and then do-re-mi-fa-sol-la-ti-do, without stopping. She walks around putting her ear down close to listen to each of us. When she comes to me she says: 'The brother is better.' I don't like singing as much after that. When she takes the big girls for the choir I like listening to them because they are lovely singers.

One day when Miss Sarah is away Miss Hanna brings us into her classroom to teach us instead. She has all the boys standing around in a circle. She asks us what we'd like to be when we grow up. Some of the boys say: 'I'm going to be a farmer,' or, 'I'm going to a be lorry driver.' Andrew Caverly says: 'I'm going to drive an aeroplane.' I say I'm going to be a priest because my uncle is home from China and he's a priest and I'm called after him and my birthday is the same day as his. Miss Hanna says I am a very good boy. Then she asks my brother what he's going to be when he grows up. My brother says he's going to be a bishop.

Every morning my mother packs our lunch, two cuts of bread with butter and jam, and a bottle of milk each. Then we walk out the back door to school. When it is nice weather we don't bother with shoes. We can run faster without them. We go down the steps to the field below the house, and then the field after that and the field after that again until we come to the warm field. My brother says that field is always warm, even in winter when there is frost in every other field. The rabbits like running around in that field. It must be because it is always warm.

Next we come to where the flax pond used to be, and then we cross over the wire fence and walk along by the water works until we come to the foot bridge. Whenever there is a flood or if it is very frosty Johnny Noonan comes out of his cottage with a hay pike and he walks across the bridge with us. Johnny is the keeper of the waterworks and he lives with Mrs Noonan and their son Chris. Chris drives a van for Barnett's, selling clothes around the country. He is getting married to Dolly Clinton who comes from Drogheda. They met each other in the sanatorium, wherever that is.

After we cross the river we go through Willie Kingston's farmyard. Margaret Kingston comes to school with us. She has black hair and she runs very fast. Her brother Sam goes to school as well but he is the same age as my big brother.

Sometimes Dan Harnedy gives us a lift to school in his horse and butt. We don't like it because his butt has iron wheels and it takes all day to get to school, and we'll be late and Miss Sarah will get cross with us. Dan Harnedy is as deaf as a stone and he can't hear a word. It's much better when we get a lift from Jim Carthy or Paul Sam Jim, because they're not deaf and their butts have rubber wheels and they go a lot faster.

My big brother has come back to school after the accident. People ask him what happened to James. One boy asks my brother was he killed too. My father tells my brother to mind himself and not to play any rough games. He'll only go to school for a short while until he is fourteen, then he'll stay at home working on the farm with my father.

We take our time walking home after school. Sometimes we play on the road. Sometimes we watch DJ Dempsey making concrete blocks in the gravel pit. Sometimes we look into Sam Gosling's house to see if he is asleep. There are ridges in the field beside Sam Gosling's house because potatoes were sat there during the famine and they rotted in the ground and they were never dug up. Nobody has dared plough the field ever since.

We nearly always stop at Paul Sam Jim's house, because Paulie will be starting school next year. There are trees behind Paul Sam Jim's house and one of them is very high. There is a stream that you can't see but you can hear it making the noises a stream makes when it is in a hurry to get as far as the river.

There is a hazel tree before we get to Kingston's bridge. We pick some hazel nuts and try to break the shells with a stone but they are very hard. The place is called 'Carraig a Thonnaig'. It means the hill of the foxes. It's where my father used to hide during the troubles.

When we get as far as the footbridge we hold on to the wire and look up the river and watch the water coming towards us until the bridge starts moving like a ship. It goes faster and faster until in the end we have to close our eyes to make it stop. After we cross the foot bridge we climb up to the tanks of the waterworks and look in over the wall. Sometimes one of the tanks is emptied, and Johnny Noonan is digging up the gravel and pulling any weeds that have grown on the bottom. This is so that when the people in town drink the water it will taste nice and fresh. We have our own well of spring water at home and that is much better than having to drink the water the people in town drink.

Sometimes Johnny Noonan goes away in his horse and trap. He crosses the river beside the footbridge where the stones are smooth and the water is not very deep. When Johnny is away we play around the tanks. We lift open a heavy iron door where there is a ladder going down into a tank under the ground. There are big pipes in this tank and if you shout your name into the tank it makes your name sound like iron.

In the spring there is frog's jelly in the old flax pond. We wiggle it with our toes until it shivers. I try to get some of the black spots out of the frog's jelly. This is very hard to do because the jelly is very slippery. My brother says if I let them alone the black spots will be frogs themselves. Before long there are hundreds of small frogs in the flax pond. Frogs are great fun, especially small ones because all they do is jump. If you watch a big frog you can learn how to swim.

Back in the warm field there are rabbits running around, and there are rabbits' grains everywhere. They are the same size as a pea and there are so many you couldn't count them. The last few fields home are all uphill and we will have to hurry because my mother will be cross if we're late. She'll ask what kept us, and what took us all day to come home?

School Continued

Joseph O'Neill is calling me names. He's saying: 'Carty Barty pudding and pie, kissed the girls and made them cry.' I tell him to stop saying that, but he only says it again. I say I'll tell on him, and that makes him stop alright. When I go home my father asks me was there any news from school. I tell him Joseph O Neill was calling me names. I tell him he was calling me Carty Barty. My father says there's not much harm in that. He says I should stand up for myself. He asks, why don't I answer him back, why don't I say 'Joseph Neill yella meal'.

The next time Joseph O Neill says 'Carty Barty pudding and pie', I say, 'Joseph Neill, yella meal.' He says: 'I'll tell my mother.' I say: 'Ah don't, t'was my father told me to say that.'

The next day the postman brings a letter from Joseph O Neill's mother. She's complaining that I called her son 'yellow meal', and that I said it was my father told me. I'm in bigger trouble than ever now, because I shouldn't have said it was my father told me to say it. My father says to my mother: 'You'd have to be careful what you say in front of a child.' Soon after that Joseph O Neill goes to live in town, he goes to a different school now. No one calls me Carty Barty any more.

We are learning about history. All about 1916. How Patrick Pearce freed Ireland. There is a picture of Patrick Pearce in the history books. He is facing sideways. He is wearing a soldier's uniform. That is why the national anthem is called 'A Soldier's Song'. I say that my father was in the volunteers, that he fought in the troubles, that he slept out in Carraig a Thonnaig when he was on the run. Everyone who fought to free Ireland was a hero, so my father is a hero. But Philomena Young says my father was no more a hero than her backside. She says he was put in jail. She says Jerh Mack gave him the knee into the big school during the civil war. I don't like Philomena Young saying that.

The Master is teaching us today, because Mrs Fitzgerald is sick. He shows us a new stamp. He asks us who is on the stamp. Someone says Patrick Pearce. He says no. Someone else says De Valera. He says no. Michael Collins. No. In the end the master says the man on the stamp is John Barry. Then he asks us if anyone can tell him who John Barry was. Nobody knows the answer. The master is about to tell us that John Barry came from County Wexford and that he was the founder of the American Navy, when Jerome Cadogan puts his hand up. Jerome Cadogan hardly ever puts his hand up. The Master says: 'My gracious! Jerome has his hand up. Tell everyone Jerome, who was John Barry?'

'A brother to Mick, sir.'

'My gracious! A brother to Mick. And who, might I ask, is Mick?'

'Mick Barry. The bowler, sir.'

Sometimes on the way home from school we go into Dempsey's to deliver *The Far East*. Mrs Dempsey is very nice and she always gives us buns. One evening just outside of Dempsey's I stand on a big thick thorn and it goes right into my foot. I go hopping back to Dempsey's house and Mrs Dempsey calls Sonny. He tries to pull the thorn out but I won't let him go near it because it hurts too much. Then he thinks of a plan. He tells me to close my eyes, and while I'm closing my eyes he pulls the thorn out. I give a fierce scream because it hurts so much and then I carry on crying for a long time. Mrs Dempsey makes tea and gives me more buns and then she tells Sonny to take me home on the bike. I sit on the bar of his bike and he brings me all the way home. My foot is very sore and I have to stay at home from school for a week. I bathe my foot in hot water and Lysol every morning and evening. After a week my foot gets very itchy and when I'm scratching and picking at it I pull out a piece of thorn about half an inch long. My mother puts it in a saucer and shows it to everyone who comes in so they can all see how brave I was. After that I go back to school again.

My sister goes to school on a bike because she is big, and she has a new bike. She goes the long way around. You can't ride a bike through the fields because you couldn't cycle over the ditches, and anyway you'd get a puncture. One evening she says I can ride on the carrier. I can't ride on the crossbar like I did on Sonny Dempsey's bike because it is a girl's bike and it has no cross bar. So I ride on the carrier. Everything is going fine until we go past Jim Carthy's. It is downhill after that and my sister starts to go faster. As we round a corner I put one leg out to keep my balance, and I put the other leg in. My heel gets caught in the spokes and we are going so fast it takes a good while before she can stop. By this time the skin is hanging off my heel and it is very sore. When my sister sees my heel she gets an awful fright. She tells me to stop crying if I'm able, but I'm not. She goes as fast as she can, and when we get home she takes me into the car house and tells me to wait there. She wants to warn my mother there is something wrong, so my mother won't get too much of a fright. But she is afraid to say anything, and she keeps waiting for a chance to say something without giving my mother a fright. In the end she tells my mother that I came home on the bike with her and that I am outside in the car house. When my mother comes out she is mad with my sister and says: 'Look at the state of the poor child.' She washes my heel in hot water and Lysol, and then puts iodine on it. The iodine pierces my heel like mad. She then puts ointment on it and a bandage. I have to stay at home from school for another week until it gets better.

Sometimes we look into Dempsey's gravel pit. There is a man

there and he has a machine for making concrete blocks. He mixes the gravel with cement and then puts it into the machine, like putting a cake into the oven. Then he presses the cover down on it, and then lifts it out and puts it on the ground until it gets hard. When he has enough blocks made a lorry comes and takes them away. Chris Dempsey drives a lorry and he is good fun because he smokes and tells stories. Sometimes if he is going in the direction of the school he gives us a lift in the lorry. That is better than a horse and butt, because we are up high and we can see all around us. It is much quicker as well, and we won't be late for school.

Other lorries come to the pit as well to draw gravel. One time there is a driver waiting beside one of these lorries and we say hello to him. He has black hair and a cap and he is smoking a fag. He says: 'Does your father sleep with your mother always?' He says it with a kind of a cackle while he is blowing smoke out through his nose. We don't know what to say, so we don't say a bit. We didn't know there was supposed to be anything wrong with that. We thought everybody's father and mother slept together. But there must be something wrong with it the way he cackles and blows the smoke out through his nose. We ask each other afterwards, how did he know? When we get home I ask my mother why she and Daddy sleep together and she says who asked me that? When I tell her it was the lorry driver she says: 'Is that so?' We can tell she is very cross.

That night my father asks us did we know the lorry driver. We say we didn't. Then he asks us what the lorry driver looked like and we tell him he had a funny laugh and blew smoke through his nose. My mother says that if we see him again not to talk to him or take any notice of him at all. When Cyril Collins comes scoraíochting on Sunday night I hear my father asking him to find out who the strange lorry driver was.

First Holy Communion

I'll be getting my First Holy Communion this summer. We have been learning our catechism with Mrs Fitzgerald for a long time and we'll all be ready soon. Before that we will have to make our First Confession.

Mrs Fitzgerald practised confession with us to make sure we know how to do it properly. She pretends to be the priest and we tell her our sins. They are not real sins because you should tell those only to the priest. These are sins we pretend to have committed so that we can practise with Mrs Fitzgerald.

I tell Mrs Fitzgerald I have been a very bad boy, which is a lie, because I have not been a bad boy. So now I have another sin to tell the priest, because I have told Mrs Fitzgerald a lie. But it is not really a lie because I was supposed to be making it up. It's when you make something up and you're not supposed to that makes it a sin.

Fr Carmody comes to school to hear our confessions. Mrs Fitzgerald has set up the empty classroom so that Fr Carmody can hear our confessions without anybody else hearing our sins.

Fr Carmody is very deaf and we have to shout our sins out loud so he can hear them and we can be forgiven. When my turn comes Fr Carmody is wearing a black soutane and a biretta. He is sitting in his chair by the window.

I tell him all my sins and he gives me absolution. That means that all my sins are gone away and I am a perfect boy once again. I can see out the window towards Robin's Cross. There is a man with a sack on his back. He is carrying away my sins in his sack.

We go to town in the horse and trap to buy my First Communion suit. We go to the Corner House and my mother gets me to try on a few suits and then she picks out the one she thinks I look nicest in, and she makes a bargain with the man in the shop. Then she does all the other shopping and then we go home. When we are passing the creamery my father asks my mother how she got on with the suit, and she tells him she got a very nice one and that it suits me down to the ground. He says: 'I suppose it was costly?' She says: 'I had to go over the pound for it.' He says: 'Sure you'd get nothing for a pound nowadays.' She says: 'The shoes were too costly.'

The night before the First Communion my mother washes me from head to foot.

Then she lights the candle and lets me take it up to bed because Mrs Fitzgerald said it was best if the candle was used to being lit. When we get to the church the boys kneel on one side and the girls on the other. We do everything the way Mrs Fitzgerald showed us. She said the host might stick to the roof of our mouths for a little while but that was no harm. She said after receiving Holy Communion we should close our eyes and put our heads in our hands to make our thanksgiving. The other boys have forgotten to do this, but when I look at Mrs Fitzgerald she nods her head and then I know I'm doing it right. Afterwards we get a brown scapular and a miraculous medal to wear around our necks.

After the Mass we have our pictures taken and then we all go down to Frank Goggin's pub. We have lemonade and biscuits. The men drink porter and whiskey and the women drink sherry.

Afterwards we play in Frank Goggin's yard. There are horses un-tackled from their traps, and there are plenty of things to run around and jump over. We all have a great time. Then we have more lemonade and biscuits.

More Tales from School

Paulie Kingston has fallen in love with my sister's blonde hair, and the ribbons in it.

He has seen her passing in the horse and trap and he knows she will start school soon. She will be his friend, he says. They will sit next to each other, sharing a desk. He will help her with her lessons. They will play together and be best friends. His mother tempers his enthusiasm. Paulie is too young to know that being a Protestant makes everything different. Anyway, come the day he gets cold feet. We come past his house as usual and he comes out to join us. When he sees my sister at close quarters he is tongue tied and embarrassed. He can hardly say a word.

When we get to school there is a flurry of excitement. Everybody crowds around to see the new girl. The new girl is not too happy with being the object of curiosity. But it's a great day for me. I have been chosen to be in charge of her. That makes me almost a big boy. Besides, I'm nine and a half. She could have chosen my brother to be the main man, but she has chosen me. She is beautiful and I can see why everybody is so excited. Indeed,

I regard myself as being partly responsible for her beauty. She is, after all, my sister. It is my job to mind her, and I have my own private ideas about all the fun she and I will have together. It will be my job to mind her, and that is that.

The first thing is to deliver her to Mrs Fitzgerald's classroom door. We get to school early. It is not time to go in yet. What to do? I tell her wait there and the door will soon be opened. She does no such thing. As I turn away to walk down the boys' yard she follows me. She makes no accommodation for the fact that the boys play in one yard and the girls in the other. I walk over and stand by the hedge. It is still the boys' side but it is sort of neutral. Having her standing next to me at the hedge is not nearly as bad as having her follow me down the playground on the boys' side. I've never had this situation before. My day of triumph is beginning to show signs of strain.

She's looking to me for leadership, but I haven't given that part much thought. I've been concentrating on ownership. She doesn't know what to do, and I haven't filled her in. Eventually the school is open and I bring her to the door where Mrs Fitzgerald's classroom is. But she won't go up the steps. When I tell her it is time now to go upstairs to Mrs Fitzgerald's classroom she thinks that is a very bad idea.

When I get back to the entrance to the Master's room she is still following me. She kind of hides behind my back, and then when I go inside, she shoots in at a flying run and sits on a desk behind me, with her head down. She's thinking maybe the Master won't even see her. I can feel her trying to disappear into my back.

She has been told she is coming to school 'with me'. And now they want her to go somewhere else. She just isn't having any of it. And there she sits in the seat directly behind me, which leaves me powerless and exposed. Nothing like this has ever happened to me before. I'm failing miserably. It's a disaster from start to finish and there is no remedy for it. In the end the Master takes the matter in hand.

'I see we have a new girl today,' he says. He asks her name. 'Frances is it?' He talks to her nicely. He suggests she might enjoy being with the other pupils who have only started school recently and are her own age. She is persuaded by the logic of his thinking, and before too long she agrees to give it a try. This time I take her all the way up the stairs, and she decides to stay.

The next crisis is at play time. She should go and play with the girls, in the girls' yard. She's not supposed to go in the boys' yard. But that is where I am, and that is where she is determined to be. She goes looking for me, all the way down to the bottom of the yard where girls never go, instead of going to the girls' yard where boys never go.

Eventually I have to lead her back to neutral ground; the gable wall at the front of the school. She stands with her back to the wall surrounded by a crowd of pupils. Some are there out of curiosity. Others want to make friends with her. But she remains suspicious of them all. Whenever anybody comes too close she kicks them on the shins. A boy tries to explain that he wants to be her friend. She kicks him as well.

I am seriously embarrassed. I've never seen my sister kick anybody before. Still, I'm proud of her as well. She is so cute, and brave, with her blonde hair and her bright eyes, and her size nothing sandals. I won't have to mind her for very long. She'll mind herself. God help anyone who thinks she'll be easy to push around.

THE GEESE

My mother keeps hens and chickens. They sleep up in the rafters in the hen house. They lay eggs in boxes, and sometimes a hen goes off and lays eggs in a nest under the hedge. Sometimes I find a nest and I show my mother where it is because I'm a good boy and if I tried to bring the eggs in myself I might let them fall and they would break.

During the day the hens walk around and they scratch the ground because that's what they like doing. Sometimes when it is hot they sit under the fuchsia bushes. When my mother goes to feed the hens she makes funny noises and she scatters the grains around with a big sweep of her arm. The hens make even funnier noises when they run after the grains. They eat them up and then run after some more grains until the grains are all gone.

Jack the egg-man comes every two weeks and he buys our eggs. My mother has to wash them first and my sisters help her but I don't help her because I'm too small and I'd only break the eggs. He pays for them by the dozen.

The fowl house has to be properly locked, and the square hole in the wall where the hens go in and out has to be closed, in case the fox comes. He comes in the night and he tries to carry away a hen if he can catch one. My mother tells the story about a house where they forgot to close the hole in the wall and the fox came in and ate all the hens and his belly was so full he couldn't get back out the hole and he had to stay there all night, and in the morning when the woman opened the fowl house door the fox nearly knocked her down he was in such a hurry to escape. Sometimes I run into a fox below in the bog. I'm a bit frightened of him but I make a very loud noise and he runs away.

My mother keeps geese as well. We have five geese and a gander. The goose eggs are a lot bigger than hen eggs because geese have bigger bottoms. Their eggs are bigger than the size of my two fists. The eggs are a sort of green colour and they have a very strong taste. My father eats a goose egg for breakfast and the rest of us eat hen eggs.

The geese wander around the fields nice and slow and pick at whatever grows on the ground. Grass and worms and anything else they like. They make hissing noises when they don't want you to come near them. The gander is in charge of the geese. He is always making hissing noises whenever anyone goes near the geese. It is great fun to make the gander hiss when he is on the other side of the wire. Sometimes I wave at him or poke him with a stick and he gets very cross and hisses at me, but there is nothing else he can do to me, only hiss.

By this time my sister is bigger. She's well able to walk and run, and she has white hair and a ribbon in it. One day I'm minding her, and when I'm not looking she climbs under the gate and goes into the field where the geese and the gander are. The geese take no notice of her but when the gander sees her he starts hissing like mad and running after her. The first thing I notice is I hear my sister screaming, and then I see her out in the middle of the field and the gander running after her. The next thing she stumbles and he's standing on top of her and taking bites out of her. I don't know what to do so I run in home as quick as I can and shout to my mother that the gander is killing Frances. I'm so frightened I can't get my breath and my mother doesn't know what I'm saying and the gander will have my sister killed. My mother tries to calm me down so she can make out what I'm trying to say, but the more she tries to slow me down the worse I get. All I can think of is the gander killing my sister. And it's all my fault because of the way I've been vexing him with the stick through the wire. In the end my brother runs out and frightens the gander away and brings my sister out of the field. My sister isn't even crying but I'm in an awful state.

After that I keep well away from the gander. My brother says I'm frightened of him, and I say I'm not, but I am. I hate the gander for the way he tried to kill Frances and every time I see him in the field, or whenever he looks at me through the wire and hisses, all I can think of is him standing on top of my sister and biting her hair and trying to pick her eyes out.

He's nearly as bad as Mahony's dog. Mahony's dog is very cross and he doesn't like me. Whenever I go to their house for a message he starts barking as soon as I come around the corner, and when I shout at him to lie down or if I wave a stick at him it only makes him worse. Mrs Mahony says he won't bite me at all but I know he will. A stick is no good because he might bite the stick and pull it out of my hand and then he'd go for my legs. A stone is better than a stick, so I find a stone to have ready in my pocket. And then I see a better stone so I pick that up as well. By the time I get to Mahony's my pockets are full of stones. I throw one at him and it misses, and before I can get another one out of my pocket he is almost on top of me. When Mrs Mahony says he doesn't bite that only makes it worse. She says he never bit anyone yet, but what good is that because I'm the only one he wants to bite.

One day my mother says we'll have to get a new gander. She says the one we have is too old. I'm glad because maybe the new gander won't hiss at me and be cross and I'll be able to go into the field whenever I like. The new gander is smaller than the old one, but you have to look very carefully to see which is which.

They have the same colour beaks and they walk the same. The new gander has nothing against me.

The old gander won't let the new gander join in. He hisses at him and he won't let him near the geese. He makes him pick the grass all by himself. Every time the new gander comes anywhere near the geese the old gander drives him away. In the evenings when the geese come home they walk up the field in a line, the gander leading and the geese following. The new gander walks about twenty yards behind. He looks frightened and lonesome.

One evening I look out the back window and see the first gander leading the geese as usual, and the second gander following about twenty yards behind. I'm looking at them for a while before I notice there is something vaguely different. I can't put my finger on what it is. Then it hits me. The new gander is walking in front and the geese are following him. It is the old gander who is walking about twenty yards behind, and it's he who looks frightened and lonesome now. The new gander is my hero. But I can't help feeling a small bit sorry for the old gander. The next week my mother asks Jack the egg-man to take him away.

Rabbits and Other Animals

I never saw a badger. They're supposed to be very cross and if you met one they'd bite your leg until it broke. I hope I don't meet a badger. I don't like weasels either, because they'd follow you home and suck your blood while you were asleep. PJ Hayes said that at school. I saw a dead weasel one time. He was lying by the ditch in the briar field. He was lying on his side and he had one eye open. I couldn't see the other eye and I was frightened to touch him. I was afraid the rest of the weasels would get my smell off of him and think it was me that killed him. They might follow me home like PJ Hayes said they would, and suck all my blood.

I'm not a bit afraid of rabbits. I see them running around in the fields every morning. They live in burrows in the ground. Big people don't like rabbits. My father says a horse could put his foot in a rabbit hole and break his leg. You might be mowing a field of hay or cutting corn and the horse's leg, or the wheel of the mowing machine, could go down the hole and where would you be then? But I like the look of their white furry tails, and the way you wouldn't have to be afraid of them.

South in Miah Neill's there are black rabbits. I bet PJ Hayes never saw a black rabbit. I had a rabbit of my own one time. He was a small rabbit. I found him in the ditch in the field behind the house. I brought him home and made a bed for him in the big kettle behind the small door. It was a kettle that wasn't being used for anything else and it was the right size for a small rabbit. I made the bed of soft hay, and then I brought him blades of grass to eat. He didn't want to eat the grass while I was looking so I put them into the kettle next to him so that he could eat them whenever he got hungry. I put the cover on the kettle to keep him warm, and to keep him from going astray and maybe the cat or the dog eating him. The dog or the cat wouldn't know he was my rabbit and that they were not supposed to eat him. My plan was that we would become friends and that by the time he was grown up we would be such good friends that he would want to stay with me and we would be friends always. Like the two boys Romulus and Remus who were looked after by a wolf and then built Rome when they got big, and the wolf was always their friend.

I showed my rabbit to anybody who came to the house. One day Padraig Scartha came. He was a man of the roads that came and slept in our settle for a night whenever he was passing. He wore black clothes and a hat and he slept in his clothes on the settle. My father said: show Padraig the rabbit. So I showed Padraig Scartha the rabbit and told him how I fed him with blades of grass. Padraig Scartha said: 'He's a fine little rabbit,' and he rubbed him on the back. The next day I found the rabbit dead inside in the kettle. I told my mother that Padraig Scartha broke his back when he rubbed him with his hand. My mother said that was hardly the cause of it at all, but I knew it was. After that I looked for another rabbit but I couldn't find one that small.

My brother showed me a hare once. A hare is like a rabbit except he has very long back legs and his ears are longer than a rabbit's. He can run very fast and jump when he's running. Big people don't mind hares because they sleep on the ground and they don't dig burrows in the field. Hares are not as plentiful as rabbits so they're not all over the place. You'd be walking along fine and easy and the next thing a hare would jump up from the grass and run away like mad across the field.

I'm afraid of the fox as well. The fox is about the same size as a dog but he can run fierce fast. My brother says there is no need to be afraid of the fox because the fox would run away as soon as he sees people. I got a big fright one day when I was going down the boreen towards the river. The fox jumped over the ditch and landed right in front of me. I gave a fierce screech to see if I could frighten him away before he saw that I was frightened of him. He ran away as soon as I screeched.

The other thing I never saw was a water dog. PJ Hayes says that if you put your leg into the river and there was a water dog in the river he'd take your leg off with a single bite. The good thing about a water dog is they wouldn't get your smell and follow you home like a weasel. They stay in the river all the time and they live under the water. That's why I have never seen one. My uncle says a water dog is no harm at all. My uncle says a water dog would never bite people. They mind their own business and they only bite fish. I keep looking into the river to see if there is a water dog but I've never seen one. I bet PJ Hayes has never seen one either.

The Master

I'm in the Master's room now. I'm big enough to be one of the big boys. The Master is very old because he has a bald head. Every day for his lunch he has a raw egg. He brings it in a cup and when it comes to lunch time he puts it back on himself. When he lifts up the cup and puts it to his mouth his eyes turn out as if he was watching two opposite corners of the sky, and then he throws his head back and down it goes. We can see his throat widen when he slugs it. We can almost see the bulge as the egg goes down the inside of his throat. When it is gone all the way down he blinks and lets out a big breath, like a man downing a glass of whiskey at a wake, except he doesn't make a noise.

When he is teaching us he walks back and forth. Sometimes he puts his hand on the rostrum and stands there telling us things. He only goes up in the rostrum when he has something very serious to say, or when he is filling in the book with all our names in it. Some days he gets cross with us and he says he's going to give someone 'a thrashing'. When he gets very cross he says to one of the big boys: 'Go out and cut me an ash plant.' Sometimes he slaps people with the stick, but not very often.

I should be doing my sums but I like listening to the Master when he is telling stories in history to the bigger boys. All about Brian Boru and how he defeated the Danes in the battle of Clontarf. Defeating someone is beating them, only worse. When the Master is finished, he starts asking questions to make sure they were listening and that they remembered it. He asks them: 'What did Brian Boru do when the battle of Clontarf was finished,' and no one knows the answer. In the end Jerome Cadogan says that he went home and had his supper. So I put my hand up and the Master says: 'My gracious, yes boy,' and I say, he did not because he was dead. Late in the day when he was in his tent saying his prayers a Dane crept up and killed him with a sword. They had the battle as good as won by that time, and the Danes never came back to Ireland after. That was a good thing because they were always robbing the monasteries, and the monks were having to build round towers up into the sky so that they could climb into them and pull the ladder up after them, and the Danes couldn't follow them and steal their chalices that were made of gold. The Master says: 'My gracious, that boy is putting you all to shame. If only he would stop dreaming.' I like history a lot better than sums.

Siobhan Mc Cormick is a lot older than us and she is still at school because the Master is helping her to prepare for an exam. Mike Crowley is way older than us. He is a big man and he is learning how to be a guard. He is related to the Master.

In cold weather the Master sits near the fire with his back to it, correcting people's lessons, and sometimes he goes to sleep. Pat Collins laughs when he gets his copy book back because there is a line where the Master's pen slipped when he fell asleep.

The Master tells us a story that happened in another school. The Master in that school used to smoke a pipe and one day the inspector came and the Master had the pipe filled and lit and the inspector was in the door on top of him before he knew it. So he pretended to be giving a lesson on how to smoke a pipe. Well, not how to smoke it exactly, but to explain to them how a pipe works and why the smoke goes one way and then the other when you put it in your mouth and smoke it. The Master is delighted that the Master in the other school made a fool of the inspector.

KILLING THE PIG

We're going to kill the pig on Tuesday because he is plenty fat enough now. Tomorrow we must ask the Master to be let home early from school. The Master says that killing a pig is no reason for going home early and he has no doubt they'll manage to kill the pig without us. My father says: 'What do the Master know about killing pigs?' He says he has a good mind to keep us at home from school for the day. But he doesn't in the end. So when it comes to Tuesday we have to run like mad to get home in time for the killing. We get home in the fastest time ever.

The first thing we have to do is take off our school clothes because there is going to be blood everywhere once they start. My father is edging the big knife on the edging stone and every little while he strokes the blade with his thumb until he is satisfied that it is edgy enough.

When we're ready, my uncle ties a rope around the pig's snout and she is brought out of the pig house on a long rope. They drag her screaming onto the flat flagstones behind the water tank. By this time my uncle has shortened the rope and the men grab hold

53

of the pig and knock her down and turn her over on her back. They kneel down at each side of her holding a leg each. The pig is making a fierce noise. You can hear her screeching miles away.

Then my father gets down on one knee on the ground beside her and he makes a thin cut all the way down her throat. He runs the knife along the cut again, this time making it deeper. By this time the pig is screeching like fair hell, and you can see the pink colour of the inside of her throat. When the cut is good and wide my father changes his grip on the knife so the point is facing straight down. He steadies himself and then he gives one almighty plunge and the knife goes deep into the pig's throat and straight to her heart. She makes one loud roar followed by a sort of gurgling, and the blood starts spurting out like mad.

This is when my mother rushes in beside the pig's throat with a large, fairly flat basin. She puts the basin beside the pig's neck so that the blood flows into it. The pig is still alive with her heart pumping the blood into the basin. When the basin is half full my mother pours the blood into a bucket, and starts again. This is where we come in. We have to keep stirring the blood in the bucket, so it won't go lumpy. It's a nice feeling to have your hands in the bucket of hot blood, and stirring it round to cool it down. It's hard to keep the blood from getting all thick and lumpy because that's what happens to blood if you don't cool it down quick. My mother keeps putting more blood into the white enamel buckets, and my brother and I keep stirring it until it has cooled. There is always some of the blood that goes into a lump in spite of us. It happened as well when we killed a pig the time before. All the same we manage to keep most of the blood from getting thick and lumpy.

By now the pig has stopped squealing, but a few gurgles still come from her throat, and she gives a class of a shake or a shudder now and then. When she does that more blood spurts out until there is no more blood to come. My mother takes the two buckets of blood inside the house. She covers them with a cloth so that no flies or anything like that will get into the blood. Later on she will start making blood pudding.

Our hands and arms are covered in blood by the time we're finished, and we like that. Some of the blood has spattered onto our faces as well. It is a funny feeling when the blood starts drying. It's like someone pinching you on the arms. My mother says to go and wash ourselves, but we like to leave the blood there as long as we can. Tomorrow we'll be telling everyone all about it in school.

The next thing is, the men lift the pig and carry her behind the house where there is a pulley set up in the yard. My father cuts a hole at the back of each of the pig's heels. They put a hook through the holes and hoist her up with the pulley. She is left hanging there by her back legs for the rest of the day.

In the evening my father cuts the pig's belly open and all her guts come tumbling out. These are put into the wheelbarrow and taken up to the yard and put on the dung heap. He cuts out her gizzards, and kidneys, and her heart separately, because they are very nice to eat. Then he cuts out the pig's bladder and tells us we can blow it up later to make a football, or a balloon. Sometimes the dog finds the pig guts on the dung heap and starts eating them. When the pig's insides are all cleaned out my father cuts some strong sally rods and sticks them into the pig's belly to keep her rib cage spread out.

Next, they wheel out the meat barrel to where the pig is hanging and pour buckets of boiling water into it. Then they lower the pig into the barrel of boiling water. That is to make it easier to shave all her bristles off. When they hoist her back out of the barrel they start shaving her. The bristles come off in big lumps. They dip her into the barrel a couple of times to keep her soft until she is shaved all over. The pig doesn't feel anything now because she is dead. She is left hanging there for the rest of the day and the night, so all the blood will be drained out of her.

The next day my father gets ready to cut her up in squares with a hacksaw and a hatchet and a knife. First he cuts her head off, and then he cuts the rest of her into quarters. Then he cuts each quarter into smaller squares. As he cuts the pig into squares he takes each square of meat and makes pockets here and there in it, and stuffs lots of salt into the pockets. Then he places the piece of meat into the barrel and cuts up some more, until nearly all of the pig is cut up and salted and put in the barrel.

The last thing he cuts up is the pig's head. He splits it into two fair halves and salts it the same as the rest. The pig's head looks funny when it is in two halves with each half having one of the eyes. You'd think the pig was still alive and looking at you, but she isn't because she's dead and she can't see anything. A good way of finding out if the pig is properly dead is to stick your finger in her eye. If she doesn't close her eye, or it doesn't get watery or anything, you know for sure she is dead.

My father keeps a few pieces of meat that he doesn't salt or put in the barrel, so that we can have fresh pork and we can give some of it to our friends and neighbours. Denis Muineag nearly always comes scoraíochting to our house after we have a pig killed. We think it's either because he can get the smell of the fresh pork from miles away and comes to see us because he likes fresh pork, or else it's because he heard the pig screeching when we killed her.

My mother makes black pudding from the blood. They are the nicest black puddings ever.

THE THRASHING

The thrashing is the most exciting day of the year. It happens in the middle of September and we have no trouble getting permission to come home early from school because the Master knows how important the thrashing is, and that we must all be there.

The first thing is the gap into the haggard has to be widened because the thrasher is too wide to fit in the gap the way it is. Then it has to be steered carefully between the stacks of corn, and holes dug in the ground so that it doesn't move while the thrashing is going on. Next the tractor is pulled into a straight line with the thrasher, and the great belt is put on the special wheel on the tractor at one end and the special wheel on the thrasher at the other end.

Then the thrashing machine man turns on the engine of the tractor and the belt starts to go around faster and faster until it makes a fierce noise, like a dog whining, only a hundred times louder. Then the men start coming from all the farms around. Some of them bring pikes and get the job of piking the sheaves from the stacks onto the thrasher, and some of them are put making the straw reek. Other men are put carrying bags of grain to the loft. A very important job is being in charge of the bags. That is watching the bags where the grain comes out of the thrasher. There is a row of about six bags attached around a class of a spout. The grain comes pouring out of these. Some of the spouts are for grains that are not very big, or where the grain is mixed with chaff. Pat Mary Anne is nearly always put in charge of the bags.

Some people bring pen knives, and their job is to stand up in the thrasher and cut the sheaves and hand them to the thrashing machine man, who feeds them into the drum. The drum is the most dangerous part of the thrashing machine. If your hand got caught in the drum it would tear your arm off, and maybe drag you into the drum altogether. If that happened you'd be killed, and the engine would have to be stopped and everybody would go home and the thrashing would never get finished. After the drum the next most dangerous part is the belt. You have to keep away from the belt because it would sweep you with it, it goes so fast.

First of all they pike all the sheaves from the stacks nearest the thrashing machine. Then they pike the sheaves from the stacks farther out, beginning with the barley. When all the barley is thrashed they stop the machine, and all the men drink porter. That is because thrashing is thirsty work. The porter is in a wooden barrel called a quarter tierce. Someone who knows how to tap the barrel so that porter doesn't burst out and go fizzing all over the place has the job of doing that. He gets a hammer and makes a small hole and then hammers the tap into the hole so the porter comes out nice and slow.

Pat Mary Ann lets us drink from his glass of porter. I don't like the taste of it much, but Pat Mary Ann says you'd get used to it. I like the way the froth of the porter makes a moustache on my lip. Pat Mary Ann has no hair on his head. I ask him what it is like being bald. He says being bald is just like being bald. He lets me put my hand on his head and it is smooth like a mushroom. I tell my brother that being bald is like a mushroom. I tell him I put my hand on Pat Mary Ann's head and that it is like a mushroom. So my brother goes and puts his hand on Pat Mary Ann's head and says to Pat Mary Ann: 'Your head is like a mushroom.' Pat Mary Ann starts laughing and tells everyone. 'Did you hear what the child said: he said my head is like a mushroom.' Everybody laughs and says: 'That's a good one alright.' We are delighted that everyone thinks we are so clever. We think Pat Mary Ann is great sport.

When the men have enough porter drank to quench their thirst my father says, 'come on men, we'll start up again.' The thrashing machine man starts up the engine and the thrasher begins kicking, and the men begin to throw the sheaves down when the stack is high, and up when the stack gets low. The men on the thrasher cut the sheaves and hand them to the thrashing machine man and he feeds a sheave into the drum and the drum gives a loud buzz and the sheave disappears. A few seconds later the part of the thrasher that is like a horse's mouth starts coughing out the straw at the other end. Four men drag big bundles of straw on their pikes to where the straw reek is being made. We watch the men making the straw reek. My uncle is in charge of making the reek. That is a very important job too because the reek will have to stand up straight so the straw will stay dry all winter to make bedding for the cattle.

After a while we go to the grain loft and watch the men pouring the bags of grain onto the heap that gets bigger and bigger. It's fun to stand in the heap and feel the grain around your legs and under your bare feet. Sometimes we hide behind the door and when a man comes in and heels the full bag of grain over his shoulder we push him into the heap and run away. Nobody minds this but one man gets cross and threatens to tell on us, so we stop doing it.

When the thrashing is all finished the men start going into the house to eat their dinner. It is a tea dinner and all the women from the neighbourhood get it ready while the thrashing is going on. There is plenty of meat for everyone. Plenty chicken and ham, and lettuce and tomatoes, and potato salad, and tea and bread. My mother says that shop bread is the handiest because you'd be baking for a week. If anyone wants more of anything they can have it. When the men are finished eating they go outside and have another drink of porter and then more of the men come in to eat. The last people to come in are the ones making the reek of straw. They have to make the top of the reek like the roof of a house so that the rain will flow down off it instead of soaking into the straw.

When everyone has had enough to eat they sit outside for a long time and drink more porter. Some people stay late into the night drinking porter and telling stories and singing songs. The thrashing machine man likes to sing a lot of songs but his voice isn't a bit good. My father says he's only a screecher. My father likes to sing too but he waits until he is asked. My father has a lovely voice. He sings 'I'll Walk Beside You' and 'The Ship That Never Returned'. Sean Neill is the best singer around here, and he sings 'Skibbereen' and 'I've met some folks who say that I'm a dreamer'. We are left to stay up as late as we like because it is the thrashing and that happens only once a year.

The Horses

We have five horses. Bob, and the grey mare, and the cob, and the race horse, and Alert. Bob has a broad back and big hooves and a hairy mane and tail. Bob is the best for ploughing because he is big and strong, and because he takes his time. The grey mare ploughs beside Bob and does other jobs with him as well, but she is not as strong as he is. She is better for going under the trap though, because Bob would only burst the shafts, and anyway he is too slow. It is the grey mare that is put under the trap when we go to Mass. The cob goes under the trap too. He is faster than the grey mare. He does other jobs as well. When Bob gets too old the cob will take over.

When Bob and the grey mare are ploughing my father gives them a feed of oats in a nose bag. He ties them to the ditch and puts the bag over their noses and ties it around their necks so that they can eat up the oats. When they are in the stable he puts the oats into the trough and after that he gives them hay. They like that. He gives them furze as well. There is a furze machine for bruising the furze beside the stable. My father shoves the furze into the machine with the hook and gowlogue, and my uncle swings the handle of the furze machine so that the wheel with the blades on each side cuts up the furze. When the furze is cut up small my father feeds it to the horses.

The race horse has a cough. He sounds very hoarse and we can hear him coughing whenever we go near the stable. My father gives him a dose for the cough but it doesn't cure him. The cough only gets worse. Then my father gives him a different dose because he thinks he has worms. My father is right because we can see the worms wriggling in the dung after him. But the race horse only gets worse and worse and in the end the vet comes, but he can't cure him either. My father says the horse will never see a race course again, that he doesn't look like he's going to get better. One morning when we come out the race horse has stopped coughing. It is because he is dead inside the stable. He is lying on his side and his front leg is sticking out straight. They have to drag him out of the stable and put him on a dray and drag him all the way down to the bottom field. He is buried in the bottom field next to the bog. He is buried near the ditch in the south corner. You can see the mound for a long time. Then the grass is thicker on his grave than it is in the rest of the field.

Alert is the stallion, and he is in the stable all the time. He doesn't come out in the field to eat grass whenever he likes like the other horses. My father or my brother brings him out on a long rope, for exercise. He runs around in a circle, and sometimes they let him go for a roll afterwards. He likes to roll in the grass and kick his legs up in the air.

People from far away bring mares to him because he is a stallion. He is famous as a trotting stallion, and my father charges three guineas every time a mare comes. Sometimes people don't want to pay him, so my father has to write a letter to tell them they have to pay. My father is good at writing letters. He says some people are the devil so slow to pay. If a mare doesn't have a foal, they can bring her back again and they don't have to pay if she doesn't get in foal the next time.

We are not let go in the yard when the mare is brought out to the stallion, not like when the bull is brought out to a cow. That is because Alert gets very excited when a mare comes in the yard, and he might break loose or kick someone dead. The bull can't kick you dead because he doesn't have hooves like Alert. He has horns though, and you should never stand in front of him. It is alright to stand in front of a horse.

When the mare is brought into the yard the big doors are closed, and then Alert is brought out to the stable door. Sometimes we watch under the door when my father and my brother and the man with the mare are too busy to notice us. The man holds the mare by the bridle. My brother holds Alert at the stable door, looking out at the mare. He holds him there for a good while until he is ready and then Alert runs out and jumps up on the mare's back.

Then Alert and the mare do the same as the cow and the bull, except Alert makes a lot of noise. He starts neighing, and he tries to bite the mare on the neck. The mare starts neighing as well, and makes almost as much noise as Alert. The bull and the cow never make any noise when the bull jumps on the cow's back. Alert has a bigger doodle than the bull, and it is a different shape as well. When he jumps up on the mare my brother has to put his doodle into the mare's backside. The bull does it all himself. The bull's doodle is long and red, and it is pointy like a carrot.

Bob is a very old horse. Sometimes my father lets us ride Bob because he is very quiet and he doesn't run very fast, and he stops as soon as you tell him.

Sometimes the trotting mares that come to Alert stay for a few days until they are in the right humour to go into the yard. Every night my brother rides whichever one of the mares are there. Gold Flake is the name of one of the trotters. She is only a pony. She is bay coloured and has a blond mane, and she can trot very fast. My brother rides her in the races at the horse show, and she nearly always wins. We all get fierce excited when Gold Flake is racing and my brother is riding her. My mother gets very excited too, but she says for God's sake not to fall off. Bluebell is another very fast trotting mare as well. When my brother is practising with the trotting mares around the field my father lets us ride Bob to keep them company. Gold Flake or Bluebell go around the field twice as fast as Bob. Bob is too old now for heavy farm work so my father decides to sell him. When my brother hears the news he starts crying for Bob because he is lonesome. I'm lonesome too but I don't start crying.

THE STEAMROLLER

There's a steamroller south near Holland's Cross. It is for tarring the road to town. The steamroller man has a caravan nearby. That way he doesn't have to go home every night, and he can start work early in the morning before people start carrying the milk to the creamery in their horse and carts. The caravan is yellow, and it is set up inside the gap into a field. I'd like to see the inside of that kind of a caravan. Not like a tinker's caravan, because they might run away with you and then you'd have to be a tinker all your life and I'd rather be the way I am.

The tinkers come around every now and then, and they mend pots and pans if people have pots or pans with holes in them. They sell combs and other things that my mother says you wouldn't want. Sometimes they ask for meat, or tea, or some bread. My mother gives them food and says: 'Clear off now so,' and they nearly always do. The women have shawls and sometimes they have babies in the shawls.

It's hard to tell if the babies are their own or if they stole them. My father says you'd have to have eyes in the back of your head, and watch everything around the house whenever they come. You wouldn't know what they'd steal right in front of your eyes, or worse still, what they'd come back to steal the day you'd be away at the cattle show.

He never said they steal children, but when I was small my big sister said if I wasn't a good boy the bad woman would come and carry me away. And then one day when my mother was gone away the bad woman came. She had a shawl around her, just like the tinker woman, and when I got frightened and started screeching and bawling my sister hunted her away up the boreen. Soon after that my uncle came and asked what all the commotion was about. I told him the bad woman came and tried to carry me away and she might come back again. My uncle says he'll make sure she'd never ever come back. But how can he make sure? He'll be gone away back to the missions and he won't be there to stop her if she comes back.

When my mother comes home in the evening I run and tell her that the bad woman came, and that she ran away up the boreen and maybe she was still there hiding in the bushes. My sister says to my mother that it was only her and my uncle having fun and that I got a fright. My mother says: 'God knows then, that was quare fun.' She is very cross with my uncle and my sister. She says they could be finding better things to be doing while she was out than frightening the child. My uncle says he is very sorry and that it was all his fault. My mother tells me not to take a bit of notice, that there was no bad woman, only my uncle dressed up in a rug. But I saw the bad woman myself, running away up the boreen.

In school the Master comes upstairs to our room and tells us there is a stranger after coming around the place, and to run away if we see him, and be sure to tell our parents about it. The Master says to be very careful and not to talk to any stranger. PJ Hayes says the stranger has chloroform, and what he'd do is put a handkerchief with the chloroform in it up against your nose so you'd go asleep straight away. You couldn't run away from him because you'd be dead asleep, so how could you run?

The Master says the stranger might be in a caravan, and if anyone sees a caravan we are to report it to him, or else tell our parents. I tell him how I saw a yellow caravan in a field near Holland's Cross and the Master says to tell my parents. When I go home from school I tell my mother there is a bad man in the yellow caravan near Holland's Cross, and that he has chloroform to put people asleep so they can't run away. I ask her what is the colour of chloroform and she says it isn't any colour, and what's all this about anyway?

On Sunday night when Cyril Collins comes scoraíochting I hear him talking about the man in the caravan. My father asks him what class of a caravan is it, and I know it's a yellow one because I've seen it in the field near Holland's Cross. When we pass Holland's Cross I show my mother where the stranger's caravan is. My father says that caravan is no harm at all. That it only belongs to the steamrolling man.

I try to look in the window of the caravan as we go past in the horse and trap, to see if there is any chloroform in it, whatever it looks like. But there is no work on Sunday and the steamroller man is asleep in his caravan. Maybe his handkerchief with the chloroform in it fell on his nose when he was in bed and made him fall asleep.

The next week the steamroller man is sitting on top of the steamroller and there is thick tar on the road and a man with a shovel is spreading small stones on the tar and then the steamroller man is rolling over it with the roller. He waves at us as we're passing and he doesn't look like a stranger although his face is all black from the tar.

CUTTING THE HAY

My father gets out the mowing machine and puts oil and grease on all the inside parts of it. Then he gets a file and starts edging the sections of the blade. Sometimes he has to put in a new section because one of them is broken and the machine won't work unless all the sections of the blade are working. When it is all ready, he tackles Bob and the grey mare and hitches them up to the mowing machine. Cutting hay is very hard work and it takes two horses to do it.

The hay is very thick and the mowing blade shines from the cutting. My father sits on the mowing machine and goes round and round the field after Bob and the grey mare until the part that is cut starts getting bigger and the part that isn't cut starts getting smaller and smaller.

There are corncrakes in the hayfield because we can hear them at night before it goes dark. The corncrakes don't like the mowing machine because they live in the middle of the hay field. They wait there until the last minute, and when the part that isn't cut yet gets down to the last narrow strip they all fly out together and away to some other hay field.

The hay will be left on the ground for a couple of days and then turned. During this time my father keeps checking the direction of the wind so that he can tell what kind of weather we're going to get. Sometimes he listens to the weather forecast on the new radio, but he says the radio man doesn't know the first thing about weather.

Magpies come in the field after the hay is all cut, and crows as well. They are looking for frogs. Some of the frogs have their legs cut off by the mowing blade and they can't jump any more, and the magpies and crows come and eat them up. Sometimes a small rabbit will get cut by the blade as well. The magpies and crows don't mind whether it's a rabbit or a frog. They'll eat anything. If the weather is very hot, the frogs that the crows don't find wither in the sun.

After we get two sunny days we all have to go out in the field and turn the hay with pikes. I have my own pike. It is not a proper pike because it is very small, but it is the right size for me. Turning hay is very hard work. Then after two more sunny days the hay has to be made up into cocks. That work is harder still. The smell of the hay makes my nose bleed and I have to lie down until it stops. My brother says it is only an excuse. He says I'm trying to dodge all the hard work. After that the cocks of hay are left there for a week of fine weather, and then we can draw it all into the hay shed. But it nearly always rains before that happens, and we have to shake the cocks of hay out in the field to let it dry again before we can draw it home.

My uncle goes up in the horse and cart and everybody pikes the hay up to him until it is a full load. Then the load is tied with ropes and brought home. My father is waiting in the shed. The hay is unloaded and then it has to be piked high up in the shed. The hay seeds get in your eyes and your hair and stick to your jumper.

GETTING OLDER

I'm getting older. I'll be ten next week. My uncle will be fifty. We'll have a joint birthday party, he says. My sister is after baking a cake, and she's going to put icing on it tomorrow. It will have sixty candles on it, fifty for my uncle and ten for me. Everybody is reminding me that I'm almost a big boy now. I like that. I like almost being a big boy. After my birthday I will be a big boy, and I'll be five years older than my sister because she's still only five.

When I woke up this morning it was the first thing I thought of. Today is my birthday and I'm a big boy at last. Then I got up and dressed and went downstairs, but nobody said a word. My brother wouldn't say a word anyway because I'm a big boy now as well as him, and he wouldn't give me the satisfaction of it, but nobody else says 'happy birthday' or even remembers. My mother is there combing my sister's hair.

My sister's hair is knotted after the night and every time the comb catches on a knot she gives a screech. My mother is trying to persuade her that it is nearly all done but my sister keeps pulling her head away and my mother says: 'For God's sake child will you stand still?' When my mother finishes my sister's hair I start walking around to see if anybody notices me. I have a smile on my face to see if it will remind anyone but that doesn't work either. I go outside and come back in, but that doesn't jog anybody's memory either. After a long time my uncle comes in from saying his prayers and my mother says: 'Happy birthday,' and then she says: 'Happy birthday,' to me too.

The big people gather around the kitchen table for dinner. I'm out back with my brother and sister. I should be in there with them. After all, it is my birthday. When it comes to the blowing out of the candles they forget to call me in, and then they remember and call me in but it's too late. Nobody cares about me.

Later my mother reminds me that James was ten when he was killed. I burst into tears. At suppertime she tells my father that I cried for James. That made it all worse. I wasn't crying for James. I was crying for me. If it was me that got killed, there wouldn't be half the fuss.

Part Two
BEYOND CHILDHOOD

FARNA (1958–1963)

$\mathbf{M}$y teenage years were mostly spent as a boarder at the Cork Diocesan Junior Seminary, Farranferris. I had often said I wanted to be a priest like my uncle. I was born on his fortieth birthday and given his name, and so it seemed a natural aspiration for me to have.

I was excited about going to boarding school, or College as my mother called it. I wanted to be a runner. I wanted to be the next Ronnie Delany. There were lots of fine runners in Cork City. They would surely be able to help me develop. I arrived in Farna in September 1958.

It was a huge shock. Such a large building to get lost in. So many other students, most of them much older than I was. The first morning I got lost coming from the dormitory to the refectory. After trying several doors that led into classrooms I opened what turned out to be the Priest's entrance to the refectory. The President was half way through the grace before meals. He stopped, his hand in mid-air, scowled at me and said: 'Get out you little rat.'

The other memorable thing about breakfast that morning was there was too much salt in the porridge. The older boys terrified me. Some of them were over six feet tall. I think they enjoyed the feeling of superiority. The College was mad on hurling, and good hurlers were looked on with awe and given special recognition.

I couldn't get the hang of Latin, and the Irish teacher frightened the life out of me. I had been the brightest in my class in the national school, but here, I could tell, I was way down the list. When it came to hurling I knew I'd be no good at that, but it didn't matter because I was going to be a runner. Training began with a lap of the big field: uphill, then downhill. Half way up the hill I found I couldn't hold my place. I was out of breath. I knew in my heart I wasn't cut out to be a runner either, but it took several years to move beyond the denial stage.

Bullying was a problem. For some reason I incurred the displeasure of the class bully, who made my life hell for the next five years. I won't name the bastard, and anyway he's been dead for years, but the remnants of my anger still reside somewhere in my body.

Corporal punishment for misdemeanours, or for failing to complete homework, or for offering a wrong answer in class was the order of the day. There was nothing exceptional in this as most similar educational institutions had the same practice. It was part of the received wisdom of the time as a good way to enhance learning, and education in general.

Not all teachers used corporal punishment, but those who did were good at it, and some of them took evident pleasure in administering it. 'You're not afraid of me,' my Latin teacher said, as he prepared to give me six strokes of the handle of a hurley on my backside. 'I am,' said I, which was the absolute truth, but in a voice I hoped would conceal the fact. I didn't want to give him the satisfaction.

Academically, I performed badly. I had low concentration levels, and wasn't that interested in academic affairs. My termly reports usually read: Attendance: 'Excellent'. (How could it be otherwise.) Behaviour: 'Good'. Application to study: 'Poor' or

'Unsatisfactory'. There was hell to pay at home. 'Why am I paying all this money and then getting "Unsatisfactory" on your report?' I dreaded those reports arriving home a day or so before the new term was about to begin. On one occasion I had received 6% for science. 'Six percent,' my mother said in exasperation. 'What is the meaning of this?' I tried to persuade her that it was six out of ten, 'because science was different.' My science teacher had advised me that my future lay in an entirely different direction. I'd be a teller of stories, though that was not how I heard his comment at the time.

I did buck up as I got older, and did enough to pass the public exams, but a couple of things seemed clear. I was no mathematician, and my flair for foreign languages was limited.

I managed to pass the Leaving Certificate, and I still had aspirations to be a priest. I did not want to be a priest in my home diocese of Cork. With one or two exceptions I didn't feel particularly inspired by the priests who had taught me.

When I met with the President to discuss my future I told him I wanted to apply to St Patrick's College, Carlow. He pleaded with me that he was expected to produce candidates for the home diocese, and would I consider going to Maynooth for the Cork Diocese?

Being flattered that they would even consider me, I tentatively agreed that he could apply to Maynooth on my behalf. But I had a trump card up my sleeve. I had failed maths in the Leaving Cert, and so was not eligible for entry to Maynooth.

So Carlow College it was to be. I was delighted with myself, though still nervous as to whether I would be accepted. Unlike groucho Marx who wouldn't join any club that would have him as a member, I would gladly be a member of any club that would have me.

A few weeks later, on an evening as I was driving the cows home for milking, my mother told me a message had come, saying that if I was going to go to Carlow I was due there the next day. I was excused from milking duties and in a mood of high excitement went to give myself a good scrub – we had running water from our own well but we didn't have a bathroom – as I anticipated my future.

Next morning, we headed for Cork City with a list as long as your arm of required purchases. Leaders Clerical Tailors was our destination. The man in Leaders Clerical Tailors saw us coming. He told us the items on the list were the bare minimum. He laid it on thick, doubled nearly everything. Black socks, black suit, black tie. White collarless shirts along with studs to attach to the Roman collar I would wear every day for the next six years.

Also required was a black hat. Only old men like my father wore hats. I kept it in a large brown paper bag to carry as hand luggage on the 3.15 train. The rest went into a somewhat battered suitcase.

Mrs Cashin, whose son Jim was in the fifth year and would make sure I arrived in Carlow safely, divided the pile into two. Half would be taken back to Leaders the next Saturday by her husband, and a refund would be obtained.

At the railway station we met some other students heading back to Carlow. The train rattled through the rich farmlands of North Cork and Tipperary, past cornfields, past the seat of the ancient kings of Munster, past the ruins of the Rock of Cashel and the blue Galtee mountains.

I wondered about what I'd done, and how it would all work out. We had high tea on the train. Pouring tea on an Irish train in 1963 was a feat requiring considerable dexterity.

Arriving at Carlow Station we were met by a man with a horse and cart, known by students as Jimmy Buckets. Jimmy was the general factotum in the College. Suitcases were loaded up and taken on board. I carried the brown paper bag with the black hat in my hand. Older students, seeing my embarrassment, playfully teased me about what might be in the bag.

CARLOW COLLEGE (1963–1969)

When I arrived at St Patrick's College, Carlow, on that late summer evening of September 1963, there was no bed available. I spent the first night in the infirmary. The next day I was given a cubicle in a part of the College called The Convents, which hadn't been occupied for several years. During the following week I was joined by a few latecomers and that became our home for the first year.

This was 1963. De Valera's Ireland. Comely maidens at the crossroads. The seminaries were bursting at the seams. As were the religious houses, male and female, as well as Missionary Orders like The Columban Fathers, Kiltegan Missionaries, African Missionaries, Holy Ghost Fathers etc. etc.

Priesthood was seen as a real career choice for the brightest and the best. In the field of sport alone, the 1962 class included the brilliant Tipperary minor hurler Len Gaynor. He would later captain and train his county to All Ireland success. Likewise, Liam Salmon from Galway would also captain and train his county to All Ireland football success. During the six years of training many found their true vocation lay elsewhere.

Life in the seminary suited me well. An ethos of support and encouragement among the student body, and the general camaraderie and affirmation, was a healing factor. 'Allow me' was a constant greeting, as in: 'Allow me to congratulate you.' I began to grow in self-esteem and self-confidence.

Daily life was regimented. First bell at 6.30am, followed by a second twenty minutes later, by which time we were supposed to be in Chapel for morning prayer and meditation, followed by Mass. We wore cassocks or soutanes, as they were called, at all times, except when playing sport or sleeping.

The training of priests had been more or less the same since the Council of Trent 1545–1563. There were high walls. These, we were assured, were to keep people out. We were free to leave any time we liked. The ethos was inward looking, lest our vocation be contaminated by the world. So no newspapers, radio, or communication with the outside world. Family events had to go ahead without us, unless they happened to take place during the holidays.

There was a college doctor, there was a nursing sister, and only in an emergency like a broken collar bone or some such was a student allowed to leave the College. There was a shop where you could buy basic items; cigarettes were in plentiful supply. The majority of students smoked. It was seen as a social hobby that helped people to loosen out. We took this regime as part of what was required to become a good priest.

On Sunday's we slept in until 7.30am. On the first Saturday we were advised by the prefect of junior house, John Calnan, that Solemn High Mass would be celebrated at 11.00am in the senior chapel on Sunday morning. If we had soutanes and surplices we were to wear them. If not, no worries, we'd have them tailored in due course.

A few minutes before Mass began Tom Gowing and Billy Hughes, newly arrived like myself, walked into the senior chapel with the choir stalls facing each other, wearing surplices over their suits, as they didn't have soutanes. It was a moment of high comedy. The supressed laughter was of a high octane just before the Solemn High Mass was about to commence.

On Wednesdays we had a half day. Students were expected to go on a walk out beyond the town of Carlow. We were to walk in groups of not less than three. This is where the black hats came in. Walking canes were in fulsome supply. We were supposed to be gentlemen now, and this is how gentlemen look. So each Wednesday with black suits, black ties, black hats and walking canes we walked the country roads outside the town. The famous Carlow dolmen was often our destination and turning-back point.

Sport played a huge part in the daily routine, several matches taking place on different pitches. Taking part was highly commended. Team games were hotly contested. Gaelic football, hurling, soccer, occasionally rugby. And a curious hybrid of squash and handball called 'moppers'. I participated in all of them with enthusiasm but with little skill.

Competition was ferocious, especially on St Patrick's day when the interprovincial finals were played. Murder and mayhem is only slightly exaggerating what took place in those encounters. If you had a physical confrontation with a student inside the College the rumour was that you'd be out the door by the next day. If you failed to stand up for yourself on the field of play it was seen as cowardice and a weakness of character.

Lectures were in English, though most of the textbooks were in Latin. The different subjects – philosophy, cosmology, epistemology, logic – sounded strange and took some getting used to. When the exams came round, written and oral, they caused the usual palpitations.

On Sunday nights there might be a movie, or a debate, or some other social activity. There were music and various other societies you could join. I found Carlow College a well-rounded, wholesome and affirming community. I found myself daring to stand up and argue a point at a debate. My self-confidence burgeoned in those first two years in junior house. There was a drama society which presented a play during term time. One such play was *An Triail* by Máiréad Ní Ghráda. We presented an English translation of the play. I was chosen to play the mother of a naïve girl seduced by the local school master, who ends up in one of the Magdalen laundries. It was my job to throw her out of our house.

Máiréad Ní Ghráda said later that in 1964 she would never have got the play into production had it been written in English. I was commended for my acting skills. I was later chosen for parts in other productions during my time in Carlow. It is my belief that I learned to be myself while pretending to be someone else.

After two years we moved from philosophy to theology. We were now in senior house. Seniors and Juniors were not allowed to consort except on special days, when 'a mix' was in place. These usually happened on feast days and other special occasions.

The Second Vatican Council was now in full swing. There was much talk of major changes in the church. The priest might one day face the people while celebrating Mass. The Mass might one day be celebrated in the vernacular. Priestly celibacy might become optional. These were some of the daily conjectures. Attitudes within the College also loosened up. Newspapers were provided. Television sets were installed in the common rooms.

Until then, and for hundreds of years, Thomas Aquinas (1225–1274) had been the bedrock of Catholic theology. Now, new and unfamiliar names were emerging from Rome. Bernhard Haring, Karl Rahner, Hans Kung, and several others were making their mark in the Council Chambers. Their influence began to make itself felt on the seminary curriculum.

The chair of the debating society put up a notice for the forthcoming debate that read: 'Should auld Aquinas be forgot, and never brought to mind.' The College was changing. It was no longer inward looking, no longer afraid of being contaminated by 'the world.' We were invited to discuss lecture content to get a better grasp and a more personal understanding of the subject matter.

A number of professors, PJ Brophy in particular, told us we were on the cusp of great changes in society and in the church. For assignments he often asked us to read novels by writers such as John Steinbeck, Carson McCullers, Flannery O'Connor, Thornton Wilder, and then write an essay on what we made of the novel in question. Though my academic marks were average, I developed a deep love for literature which stayed with me for the whole of my life. Some years ago, I wrote the poem below in his memory.

Killeshin Churchyard

(i.m. PJ Brophy)

He's buried close to the main door
so people can pass his spirit going in
and coming out. But a friend says the headstone
should be upright, reach high into the air, be visible
over the surrounding fields. It should look out loftily
and have that panoramic view he brought to everything.
Its crossbeam should evoke the wingspan of some great bird
to emphasize his vision, and the all-embracing nature of his mind.

He taught theology through the medium of novels.
The Grapes of Wrath. The Ballad of the Sad Café.
The Heart is a Lonely Hunter. The Bridge of San Luis Rey.
Going inside to pray, this friend
finds the church set up for a wedding.
Flowers all over, and remembering how
PJ loved flowers of every kind – and seeing
his grave has none – it doesn't seem right somehow.
He gently steals around, and even-handedly
from each arrangement collects a contribution.
A rose. Two lilies. Chrysanthemums. Sprigs
of Cornflower – deep pink and vivid blue.
Honeysuckle, Mock Orange blossom.
Gypsophila for its soft white haze.
Rosemary for remembrance.

Time moves on, and before we know it final decisions about ordination to the diaconate have to be made. Three of our class decide not to proceed. On June 7th 1968, along with twenty three companions of five years standing, I am ordained Deacon. It is a moment of incomparable joy. Forty years on I wrote this poem.

The Morning Bobby Kennedy Died

The Dalmatics, red, gold, purple, off white
have been allocated in pairs. Steve and I
get the green ones. Eamonn and Billy
are in red. Dr Seeldrayers is giving the organ
full throttle as we process in. The ceremony
lasts two hours, and when we come back out
it's done. We're in it now for the long haul.
Next year will be Ordination proper.

Mc Mahon with the rust-coloured hair
is at the door offering congratulations.
'Allow me, Mick.' 'You're allowed.'
A few of the boys have lit up with relief.
I'm smiling in the afterglow of it.
The organ has followed us outside
mixing in with the smell of laburnum
and cut grass. The sky is overcast.
Someone says Bobby Kennedy is dead.
I didn't even know he'd been shot.

That summer I visited Leeds Diocese for the first time. I spent three weeks as a deacon with Canon Frank Holdright at St Anne's Parish in Keighley. I found the Yorkshire accents incomprehensible, as indeed they found mine. I spent a further two weeks at the

Diocesan Pastoral Centre at Woodhall near Wetherby. Fr Michael Buckley, who had signed me for the diocese five years earlier, ran a course for deacons.

We visited such places as St James Hospital, Yorkshire Television Studio, and Wetherby Borstal to give us some experience of what serving as a priest in the diocese would be like. On the Saturday we saw Leeds United play at Elland Road. I went back for the final year to finish my studies. I looked forward to returning as an ordained priest the following year.

7TH JUNE 1969

Our final year at the seminary was quite different from the previous ones. Things had loosened up a great deal. There was much more contact with the outer world and, as deacons, we were given more responsibility. Some people in our class had got into a bit of trouble the previous year. A card school had developed. Which was not itself a problem, but staying up most of the night, and not showing for morning prayer, was.

We are supposed to give a good example to the younger students. We must cultivate a certain gravitas, try to behave accordingly. We take our turn preaching at Mass, in the College and in the local convents. We also practise celebrating Mass, which by this time is in English. We have tutorials on the administration of the Sacraments, on hearing Confessions, and all aspects of pastoral life. Towards the end of the year there are exams, called Canonicals, to see if we are fit persons to be let loose on the people of God.

There are also the practical preparations. Tailors visit the College and take measurements for new suits, cassocks, and all the clerical paraphernalia. There is a class-piece with the photographs of all the Ordinands. This will hang in the main corridors of the College, and future students can up look at us and be inspired. Invitations are sent to family and friends. Music and liturgy are prepared for the Ordination Mass. The day draws near quickly.

My father, who is seventy five, says it is way too far to travel, but he just wants me to invite him personally. I do so by telling him it is all arranged that he and Mammy are booked in to Lizzie Dunne's house. Lizzie is a very old friend of my sister Kathleen whom my father has always liked. Reassured that I want him to be there he is full of enthusiasm.

We're each allowed an allocation of tickets for the ceremony. My aunt can't find hers and goes into a panic. My uncle – the Missionary Priest – gives her his seat, then goes off and finds a chair, climbs over the altar rails and plants himself in the middle of the sanctuary.

The Ordination ceremony is a very solemn and moving affair. We lie prostrate on the floor. Each one's name is called. We answer: 'Present'. The Bishop addresses us with a question, the answer to which is: 'I am ready and willing'. He lays hands on our heads and anoints our palms with the oil of Chrism. This is the moment of Ordination. My father cries all the way through the service.

Afterwards we have a meal for family and friends in Kilkenny. It is a beautiful evening as we head home. I swim in the sea at Dungarvan. The bracing water helps me unwind. Tomorrow morning I will celebrate my First Mass.

Part Three
A CHINK OF LIGHT

James Keefe (1702–1787)

Founder of Carlow College, 1782

He sits at twilight, the light fades before his fading eyes.
The colours on the clouds turn to blood, but he can't see them.
He can hear the bird sounds as they settle into silence, in tune
With the Earth's turning, with the promptings of the heart.

He recalls those early years, from Hedge School to Sorbonne,
The streets of Paris, Notre-Dame, the ripples on the Seine at night.
A Bishop died here in '33. The message read: Mrs Kildare and Leighlin
Is become widowed by the death of our brother Mr Bernard Dunne.

In '37, James Gallagher run out of Raphoe, someone mistaken for
        him shot.
The capture of a priest is set at fifty pounds, much more for a Bishop.
In '43, nine priests arrested in Queen's County. After his consecration
        in '52,
Fr Taaffe, taken from Mass-house Lane, Carlow, sentenced to
        transportation.

Fr Nicholas Sheehy hanged at Clonmel in '66. For murder.
Things are calmer now, people keep to their own side of the road.
His address still reads: Mr Patrick Keeffe, Shopkeeper, Tullow.
His letters: datum in loco nostri refugii ... from our place of refuge.

How many have known his real identity? He has learned to walk
On tiptoe through the tangled grass, taken refuge in the shadows.
He has seen the gradual change, the slippage of the penal laws,
And now a chink of light. Limited Catholic education.

He thinks he's going to do this thing. He'll sleep on it. Dan Delany Supports him. He's the only one. The rest think it's an act of folly. He sleeps well. The sky brightens, bird sounds thicken in the air. He'll visit Fishbourne today, take the lease on Winnet's Field.

CARLOW COLLEGE

Carlow College opened on 1st October 1793. It was Ireland's first Catholic third-level college and second only to Trinity College, Dublin. The teaching faculty included three French emigrant priests who had fled France after the revolution.

Carlow College alumni include many in the College's long history who bore a great influence both in the church and in secular life. Among its most illustrious early alumni were contemporaries John England and John Joseph Therry. Their influence in shaping the infant Catholic church in the United States of America, and in Australia, is incalculable. They both hailed from Cork but were different in almost every other respect.

England, a towering intellect, prolific preacher, writer, organiser, seemed blessed with a multitude of gifts. Born in Cork City on 23rd September 1786, he entered Carlow College in 1803 and was ordained in 1808. He was a champion of Catholic Emancipation and a close friend of Daniel O'Connell.

In 1820, he was named Bishop of the new U.S. diocese of Charleston which consisted of three States: South Carolina, North

Carolina, and Georgia. The outstanding Catholic Bishop of his time founded the first Catholic newspaper: *The United States Catholic Miscellany*.

In 1826, he was invited to address the U.S. Congress, the first time a Catholic cleric was so honoured. For two hours he explained the doctrines of the Catholic church to an audience in the House of Representatives which included President John Quincy Adams. The first Catholic Bishop to articulate a separation of church and state, he was a champion of civic and religious rights. He died worn out from his exertions at the young age of fifty-five on 11th April 1842. His story is well covered elsewhere and will not be dealt with further here. His collected works were published in seven volumes in 1908.

John Joseph Therry was a street fighter. The first official Catholic chaplain to the colony known then as New Holland, he spoke truth to power. He called a spade a spade, and on occasion called it a shovel. He stood up for the poor, the prisoners, and those condemned to death. He was beloved of the downtrodden and became known as the Apostle of Australia.

John Joseph Therry (1790–1864)

Massacre at Carlow

She took and kissed the next flower thrice and softly said to me –
'This flower I found in the Wicklow hills, in Glenmalure,' said she.
'The name I call it is Michael Dwyer, the strongest flower of all,
And I'll keep it fresh beside my breast though all the world should fall.'
   – From the ballad of the 1798 rebellion, 'The Three Flowers.'

When I walk down Tullow Street I can smell the smoke
And the burning flesh. It was seventeen years ago this week,
I was only eight. I imagined it all on Shandon Street,
The yeomen firing the houses and the rebels running,
Flames streaking out of their hair and clothes
And Commander Dennis shouting: 'Spare no man.'

When my father told us about it my mother asked him to stop.
'You'll give them nightmares.' But he said we had to know
What happened, to make sure it would not happen again.
I picture them at the Potato Market, their pikes gleaming,
Their eyes alight, and Hayden going around in a whisper,
Telling them: 'Carlow will be ours before the morning.'

Come the morning they were slaughtered.
Massacred by gunfire and shot. Running into
The houses down Tullow Street, being burnt out
And bayoneted, I still cry at the thought.
It was never found out who opened the College gates
Or whether, as was claimed, they were forced.

It was whispered that one of the French priests,
Mr Chabaux or Mr LaBrune, was capable of it.

They had seen the like before, in Paris. Mayhem,
Bloodshed, Beheadings. This was not new to them.
Five hundred rebels escaped that night and lived
To fight again at Wexford and Vinegar Hill.

The rest, God help them, dumped in the Croppy Pit.
The torture and hangings went on for weeks.
Paddy the Pointer was brought in here four times.
He could point out no one. They would have liked
To close the College down. They had no legal right.
It was lucky they didn't send it up in flames instead.
Like every boy in Cork who had a father like mine
I would step into the ranks when my turn came.
Michael Dwyer was my hero, more than Emmet
Or Tone. The way he held out for five long years
In the Wicklow mountains. Sleeping in that cave,
Wrong footing the yeomen time after time.

That's what I would do when I was old enough.
In the end, there was an agreed surrender,
But they broke their word. Instead of a free passage
To America, they transported him to New Holland
Where he is today. My hopes and plans have changed
But not that much. Talking to John England has brought me here.

'Forget about armed rebellion,' he said. 'There are better ways.'
So here I am, a rebel all my life if God spares me. I can't watch
Harm being done. My father gave me that, my mother too.
Mostly I stand my ground, refuse to budge. It's got me
Into trouble more than once. 'Calm down,' the lads tell me,
But there are times I can't. The truth must never be put aside.
The President had me in the other week. He told me

My temperament gave cause for concern. Professor Doyle
Is the teacher I admire the most, a friend of Daniel O'Connell.
Peaceful agitation, look for what can be done within the law.
Argue our way. No more bloodshed. I can live with that,
Though Michael Dwyer will always be my man.

Student Report

John Joseph Therry, April 1815

Rev'd President,
Thank you for your report on student John Joseph Therry
Received on the 11th inst. While I disagree with nothing –
It is exactly as you say it is – I wish instead to offer
An interpretation which looks in an opposite light.

Therry is without question headstrong and stubborn,
Outspoken to a fault, argumentative and contentious.
He is oversensitive in his emotions, sees a slight
Where none exists, and lacks sensitivity to others.

May I say in mitigation, he is as yet a young man.
He also hails from the city of Cork, where thriving
Against the odds is a necessary rule of survival.
You add that he is blunt and without nuance.

That too, I am sorry to say, is undoubtedly the case.
My concern regarding his suitability for Holy Orders
Echoed yours exactly when I first came to the College.
I have, since that time, profoundly changed my mind.

I've watched closely and noticed, he argues only
With those above him. You, for example, or me.
He does not take advantage of anyone beneath.
The opposite in fact, he stands up for such.

While disputatious in the extreme and takes correction
With bad grace, he does have a passion for the weak,
And is fearless in the face of those who exercise power.
He will not let a perceived wrong go unchallenged.

I have watched his development these last two years.
He is ferocious on the field of play; I have noticed
When facing opponents blessed with superior skill
Or physical advantage he refuses to yield an inch.

May I humbly suggest, knowing that his preference
Is for a missionary assignment, with a leaning towards
Those who have been forced to leave their homeland,
Transported for moral failings or political engagement:

Who better to stand up for those deprived of justice,
Birth-right, loved ones, Religious Faith itself, and who
Languish in a hostile climate ten thousand miles away?
Therry is indomitable. He will not fail to take their part.
I remain,
Your humble servant,
Professor James Doyle.

The Janus

The Janus sailed from the Cove of Cork on the 5th December 1819.
On board were 105 female prisoners and 26 children,
Rev. Philip Connolly, and Rev. John Joseph Therry.

Questions were raised as to the conduct of the
Captain and crew towards
The female prisoners.

Note: On arrival, Governor Macquarie ordered an investigation. Among those interviewed were two convict women, Mary Long and Lydia Esden, Rev. Philip Connolly, and Rev. John Joseph Therry.

Captain Mowatt

17th June 1820, found poem

In regard to the Evidence of The Reverend,
A Priest of the Roman Catholic religion,
I must beg to observe that it was given with
A peculiar invidiousness regarding me, but with
A determination to represent as absolutely blameless
All those of his own persuasion.

It seems that some intercourse did take place
But there is no evidence whatsoever, that
I either assisted or connived at the Act,
Or indeed knew of it.

The Bench will not lose sight of the opinion
That it was utterly impossible for me
To totally suppress the vice.

In regard to the accusation of having
A female, Mary Long, as a constant
Companion in my berth place,
I most unequivocally deny it.

She is the female who washed for me
During the voyage and was necessarily
Sometimes in my cabin; but I protest

That it was merely for the purpose of
Obtaining my linen to wash and mend,
Or bringing them back to me when done;

In the same manner as Mary Ore, Isabella Irvin
And Ellen Molloy gave their Attendance
On the two Reverend Gentlemen.

The Voyage

The day before we were due to sail
I was a bag of cats. I would let no one near me.
My father was quiet, my mother hovering
Around the edges, sniffling, trying to get close.

I hate goodbyes. I am alright at giving sympathy,
I'm not good at taking it. I did give her a proper hug
Before I climbed the ladder. I let her cry on my shoulder.
Her last words: 'We will not see you again in this life.'

The ship looked solid enough, but when we got on board
The sight of the poor women and children in cages
Got the better of me. Captain Mowatt called us
Up on deck before we sailed.

He told us the journey would be arduous
With many hazards. Our first landfall would be
Rio de Janeiro in six weeks or so. We could expect
To sail into Botany Bay in about five months.

We had a choice: make it easier or harder for ourselves.
A well-run ship I thought. The captain is clearly a man
Of authority, with no little charm. How wrong I was.
The Mizen was barely out of sight before it started.

The captain invited Mary Long, 'to do his washing.'
She being the best-looking woman on board, and
With a wandering eye. Two weeks into the voyage
The barrier locking the women in at night was breached.

A blind man could see what went on. I challenged the Captain
On the question of immorality. He told me I was imagining it.
Over the following weeks I challenged him a number of times.
I had to give up in the end, it being a complete waste of time.

Meanwhile the nightly concourse continued. After we sailed from Rio
It got worse than ever. There was not even the pretence of good order.
Each crew member had taken one of the women to his personal service.
Some of the women were clearly carrying a child. Mary Long included.

When Governor Macquarie asked if I had anything to add,
I said I did. I pointed out to him how difficult it is
To wash clothes in the dark, and how impossible
To conceive a child by washing clothes.

Governor Macquarie to the Rev. John Joseph Therry

3rd November 1821, found poem

I receive from your hands with much pleasure
The very handsome silver trowel now presented to me;
And I feel myself very honoured in having been selected
To make use of this instrument in laying the first stone
Of the first Catholic Chapel to be erected in Australia.

It has been a great gratification to me to witness and assist
At the ceremony now performed. I beg you will accept
Of my best acknowledgements for the sentiments of
Friendly regard and kind good wishes you have been
Pleased to express for myself and my family.

Laclan Macquarie,
Governor-in-Chief.
New South Wales.

Crossing the River

The water was as torrid as I had seen it all winter.
A dog would not swim across it. I could tell
By the black cloak and the square set of his jaw
As he sat forward on the horse, it was Mr Therry.
The horse, either most stubborn or else frightened
Wouldn't so much as put a hoof on the riverbank.

We had seen him this way before, bound for Emu Plains.
Some poor misfortunates there, waiting for the rope.
He tried a dozen times but the horse just reared up.
'You won't do,' I shouted to him. 'Have you a rope?'
He asked. 'I know the whereabouts of one,' I said.
Off I went and when I came back I had a good one.

I brought four men, including young Mc Carthy
Who had strength and a good throwing shoulder.
We tied it to a tree and the lad flung it across.
Therry tied it around his chest and went in the river.
We pulled him from the bank and kept the strain.
At one point, mid-stream his head went under –

But he came up again. No sooner out of the water
He gave us the cloak to squeeze, asked to borrow
A horse which he'd swop again on the way back.
The horse shuddered down his flanks when he felt
The wet weight on his withers. Mr Therry came by
Two days later with a bad cold on his chest.

John Therry to Governor Darling (I)

20th July 1824, found poem

Sir,

At the commencement of General Darling's administration,
I did propose to his Excellency my willingness to take charge
Of fifty of the Aboriginal youth, on condition that the Government
Would supply them with provisions, clothing, and other necessaries,
And that I should not at any time thereafter, require any salary,
Or advantage, whatever, directly or indirectly;

And I had the honour to receive His Excellency's official assurance,
That as soon as the general circumstances of the Aboriginals should
Be taken into consideration my offer should then be considered;
And as that time has long since arrived, and no communication
On this subject been received by me, I have reason to apprehend
That my offer and His Excellency's promise has been forgotten.

Therefore I am induced again to submit, as I now do,
My offer to the favourable consideration of our humane
And excellent Governor, and to add in the event
Of that offer being accepted, I shall with great pleasure,
Either give five acres adjoining the Liverpool road chapel
As a place for their residence and education, or provide
Pro tempore an asylum free of rent on the chapel ground.
I have, &c.
J. J. Therry.

Prison Officer William Kelly to John Therry

14th August 1825, found poem

H.Ms. Gaol, Sydney

Rev.d Sir,

I most respectfully beg leave to acquaint you that Webb
Who is under Sentence for execution tomorrow morning
And who has been brought up in the protestant religion
Most earnestly entreated Mr. Toole, to solicit your
Attendance to give him an opportunity of confessing
And receiving the blessed Sacrament so as to
Enable him to die in the Catholic faith.

I am
Revd Sir
Your most obt servt.
William Kelly

John Therry to Governor Darling (II)

24th June 1826, found foem

For the Attention of Governor Darling

Sir, I had the honour on yesterday evening
To receive your letter of the 22nd inst. informing me
Of a complaint having been made of my having
Solemnised a marriage between a Catholic
And a Protestant, contrary to the instructions
Received from Major-Genl. Macquarie
And calling on me by the command
Of His Excellency the Governor
For an explanation.

With regard to the instructions of General Macquarie
I beg to state that I do not now, that I never did,
And never shall, consider them as imperative.
I freely admit that I thereby incurred his displeasure,
And subjected myself to the numerous inconveniences
Which resulted from it; but it was not of long continuance,

For having discovered that my refusal had not originated
From a spirit of disobedience, nor for any want of respect
For his person and Government, he received me again in his favour
As may be evidenced by some of his autograph letters now in my
       possession,
And by his public answer to my address at the Ceremony
Of laying the first stone of the Catholic Chapel.

May I then be permitted most respectfully to beg
His Excellency Lieut. General Darling, whose Government
Is distinguished for its impartiality and wisdom, who appears
To take pride in protecting the poor and the humble from the
Oppression of wealthy arrogance, that means be allowed
To Catholic parents to have their children rescued
From the fangs of voracious intolerance
From the Idol of Apostasy.

Your most obedient servant
Revd. John Joseph Therry

Governor Darling to Colonial Secretary Earl Bathurst

July 1826, found poem

Mr Therry
      Is a man of strong feelings and not too much discretion.
He is evidently disposed to be troublesome, and
Constituted as this community is,
Might be dangerous ...

He is indefatigable in endeavours to preserve his influence
Among his countrymen, and is constantly going from place
To place with this view. From the similarity of character
He can hardly fail to succeed ...

I must confess to your Lordship that I have no desire to see any more
Of the Clergy of the Catholic persuasion here ... I understand Mr
      Therry
Is acquiring wealth, and as his influence will increase with his means,
His immediate removal appears the more desirable.

I would beg to point out, that in selecting a Catholic Priest
For this Colony, it is most important that an Englishman
Should have the preference, the Catholics here
Being, I understand, nearly all Irish.

From: His Excellency Lieut. General Darling

Prison Officer to John Therry

8th September 1826, found poem

Hs. Ms. Gaol Sydney.

Revd. Sir:

I respectfully beg leave to acquaint you that
Joseph Lockett is ordered for execution
On Monday next. He is a Protestant
But wishes to die a Catholic.

I remain
Revd, Sir
Your most hble. St.
John Toole

Samuel Chipp, Prisoner, to John Therry

15th December 1826, found poem

Sydney Goal.

Reverend Sir

Wee Poor unfortunate
Men under the Sentence
of death Is verry Anxous
for you
I hope Sir
when You Resieve this

that you Will
for God Sake
not Delay
Wee do not now
the Hour nor the Moment
our Death Warrants may come.

Revd. Sir
I Saml Chipp
that is under Sentance
of death
concerning the Murder
of the Black Native

I Earnestly Wish
that your Reverence

Will make No Delay
For I am Resolved
to embrace the Roman C Faith
As Soon as you Come to Me.

Sir Wee hope
that you Will
not delay.

SAML CHIPP
JAS. MURPHY
JOHN HIGGUNS.

Prisoner John Wall to John Therry

1826, found poem

Sydney Gaol.

To the reverend Mr. terry.

Sir

There is one of the
Young men in the sells
Sadley troubled and wishes
To see you very perticler for
He bursted in teers last night
And cryed out for your assistence
So that I hope you will come to him.
John Wall
The sells – Sydney Gaol

Prisoner Charles Hunt to John Therry

6th April 1827, found poem

Prospect Road Gang.

To the Most honoured and Reverend Jhon Josep Terey Roman Catholic Clargy the Great ful thanks of Charles Hunt With that of his poor Wife and children for his Most kind and good Carrectar of him the day he was tried on the 6th of November last at th Quarter Sesons Most Reverend Sir I realy think and Ever shall think that it was the almighty God that put you in the Court that day and that yo was the Mains of My parcel sintince

Reverend Sir on that Moring Be fore I was Brough out of the Goal to Be tried I Gave my self up Entirely for Lost as Every one was telling me I wood Get Seven years and My wif 3 years but thank God th ware all Mistaken. I Never haide the Last tought of Sending to any person to Give me a Carrectar and indeed Reverent Sir I never tought of yo

But in th Moring of that day I had no place in the Gale that I could offer My Self to God But when I Got th opertunity I went in to th privey and with a Broken hart I prayed to God to Be My frind that day

So I Ever Will consider that My God put yo in th Court house that day Glory be to God most honerd Sir th Short Sentence I get is More Service to me than if I Got 7 years for by Getting 7 years I wood Give My self up for Despeare never more to meet my Distressed Wife and Children

Most reverend Sir th day you passed this place in a Gig you Most kindly told me to send you word when I wood Be nearly Laving this so I thank my God and you My time is up on th 6th of May wich day I will Be sent to Sydney

I therefore hope your Reverence will Enter feare for me and as My Wife has Got 12 months in th factory you will be the Mens of Getting her time a Medeagated Should that not be pleasing to your Reverence to Get her time Shortned I trust you will prevent me of Being kept in Government Enployment But Let me use my Endustry to have sum Relefe for her By th time She Laves th factory.

I only got a fine of Six monts so By Rite th ought have no more to Do with me Reverend Sir as you weare th means of Getting My famley so many thousand mils to joine me ower hole Depend-ains is in you Reverence to use your Enterest for hus honerd Sir

if I was a person who was Ever Brought Be fore a Judg for any Dishonesty Be fore I wood not Ever take the Liberty But as Long as I am in th Colney I never was in such trouble and it was not for thieving I was sent heer from my Neative Cuntry it was for passing one Bank note £1

and as for My poor Wife she never was in Side of a place of Confinement Be fore this nor one of her Breed I humbly hope yo will pardon th Liberty of Sending yo such a Long Letter so Most Reverend Sir I trust in God you will not Let me out of you Mind as My hole Dependance Lies in you I am Reverend Sir you Most humbl Servant

Charles Hunt

John Therry to Colonial Secretary Alexander Mc Leay

23rd November 1827, found poem

To the Hon. Alexander Mc Leay. Colonial Secretary.

It becomes my duty to have the honour
To inform you that another person died last night,
At His Majesty's General Hospital, without the benefit
Of the Holy Viaticum, which he frequently within the last few days
Most earnestly craved to be allowed to receive from my hands.

This most cruel and unnecessary privation, has been the consequence,
I am informed, of an order given to the porter of the Hospital
By Dr. Bowman not to admit me into it at any hour
Even in the absence of my brother clergyman.

If a professional infidel were to give such an order,
It might not surprise or astonish, but that a person
Who professes to be a Christian should give it,
Is to me most unaccountable.

I am not ignorant of the danger I incur by exposing
This abuse of authority on the part of Dr. Bowman,
Even to the Government, for I have reason to know
That his hostility is seldom without effect.
Your obt. Servant
John Joseph Therry

Alexander Mc Leay to Rev. Mr John Joseph Therry

January 1828, found poem

Rev. Sir

I have had the honour to receive
And submit to the Governor your two letters
Of 22nd and 23rd of this month, and am directed
By his Excellency to inform you that the Government
Cannot permit of your interfering in any way
With the public establishment.

I am also directed to add that,
As the Rev. Mr Power is the only
Acknowledged Roman Catholic clergyman
In this Colony, the Government must decline
Receiving representations from you.

I have the honour to be, Rev. Sir,
Your most obedient servant.

Colonial Secretary
Alex Mc Leay

Parramatta

7th July 1829, found poem

Having this moment learned that another victim
Has been recently added to the number of those
Unfortunate Catholics, who have been
Illegally denied the rites of their religion,
In consequence of a regulation made by
His Excellency, Governor Darling,
To exclude me from the Gaols,
The Factory and Hospitals.

I feel myself imperatively called upon
To bring this matter once more
Under the notice of the Governor,
At the risk of renewed persecution,
But still with the hope that
His Excellency's humanity,
Of which I am convinced
He is not destitute,
May induce him
To rescind it.

I have &c,
John Joseph Therry

John Therry to Governor Darling (III)

27th April 1830, found poem

Chapel House, Hyde Park.

Sir,

     I greatly regret that His Excellency the Governor
Did not condescend to direct some intimation to be given to me,
The only Catholic Clergyman in the Colony, as to the time
When the unfortunate Criminals now under sentence
At Maitland Hunters River were to be executed
In order to enable me to proceed to that place
In time to administer to them before their death
The consolations of Religion. A privilege
From which they are not now excluded
Even by the most severe and sanguinary
Of our criminal laws.

I have been this morning informed
By one of your servants
The execution is ordered to take place
On Friday next
And as the distance is only
One hundred and sixty miles
It is still possible for me
To be there on Thursday evening.

I beg to state that I shall even now
Undertake the journey if His Exe.
Order me the use of a good horse

Or any mode of conveyance
Either of land or water.

Your obt. servant
John Joseph Therry

John Therry to Governor Darling (IV)

17th December 1830, found poem

Chapel House, Hyde Park.

Sir,

      Having this morning learned that two unfortunate men
Now under sentence of death in the gaol of this town,
Are to be put on board ship, to-morrow morning,
In order to be re-transported to Moreton Bay,
And that they are then to be executed in that settlement
Without the attendance, in their last awful hour,
Of a Clergyman of the religion which they profess
And in which they wish to die, I feel it to be my duty
As their pastor, most respectfully to protest
Against this aggravated punishment, as being
In my humble opinion, both cruel and illegal.

The infliction of any punishment not sanctioned by law
Is, I presume, illegal; and to torture the mind
Is often a greater cruelty than to torture the body.
His Excellency's humanity would shrink with horror
From the bare idea of having these unhappy men scourged
On every day during their passage, no matter what good
Should be likely to result from so dreadful an example,

And yet, His Excellency has adopted an arrangement
By which they are doomed to much more severe
And perhaps most fatal punishment
Without any certainty of a good result
And with imminent danger of a disastrous one.

If a small portion of the money which has recently
Been so plentifully lavished in punishing crime,
Had been properly applied in endeavouring
To prevent it, the Colony would be more happy,
Secure, and contented than it is at present,
And His Excellency should be free from those anxieties
Which a generous and well intentioned Ruler
Must unavoidably feel under the present circumstances.

I have the honour to be Sir, With great respect
Your most obt. humbl. Servt.
John Joseph Therry

THE APOSTLE OF AUSTRALIA

John Joseph Therry served in many parishes and built numerous chapels across Australia and Van Diemen's Land. Among his many supporters was Michael Dwyer, who, when the latter died in 1825, asked John Therry to take care of his wife and children. Therry received them into his home and Mrs Dwyer became his housekeeper.

Fr Connolly had left for Van Diemen's Land in 1821, where he made little impact.

By order of Lord Bathurst, John Therry was suspended as the Catholic Chaplain and his salary of £100 withdrawn in the summer of 1826. For the next twelve years he continued his missionary work without having the official status of Government Chaplain.

The Rev. Daniel Power was appointed official Chaplain in his place in 1827. Daniel Power was in poor health. The two men did not have an easy relationship but Power was forced to accept assistance from Therry.

When Power died in March 1830, Therry was again the only

Catholic priest in the Colony. The government had little choice but to countenance his ministry. He was finally restored by the government as the official Catholic Chaplain in 1837.

In 1838 Therry was appointed Vicar General of Van Diemen's Land by Bishop John Bede Polding, the first Catholic Bishop in Australia. He visited Launchester, then Hobart, where Fr Connolly, who had sailed with him from Cork, had become estranged from his people. He reconciled Connolly before the latter's death in August 1839.

He visited the interior and attended to the convicts. He initiated the building of churches at Hobart and Launceston. He was in Van Diemen's Land when the Young Irelanders were transported there after the rebellion of 1847 and would certainly have sought them out.

John Mitchel, whose daring escape from Van Diemen's Land is chronicled in his famous *Jail Journal*, used priestly garb to disguise his identity. It is not too far-fetched to speculate that Therry might have played a part in facilitating such a disguise.

John Therry served the infant church in Australia and Van Diemen's Land for a total of thirty four years, twelve of them as the only Catholic priest in the colony. In his later years, a much mellowed man, he was given the title Archpriest Therry in 1850.

He became known as The Apostle of Australia. In May 1856 he returned to Sydney, and remained in Balmain until his death on 25 May 1864. His funeral was the biggest ever seen in Sydney up to that point.

When Pope Paul VI visited Sydney Cathedral in November 1971 his first act was to kneel and pray at John Joseph Therry's tomb.

Pope Paul VI prays at John Jospeh Therry's tomb in Sydney Cathedral, November 1971.

Part Four
A TREE CUT BACK

THE CHURCH IN THE WORLD

Meanwhile the heady days of the Catholic church in Ireland had begun to wane. The visit of Pope John Paul II in 1979 was a sort of last hurrah for De Valera's Ireland. Secular forces had begun to make their presence felt. Church attendances were already falling, and vocations to the priesthood and religious life had begun to drop.

This was also the case across the English-speaking world. It was also true of other Christian communities. But it was more noticeable in Ireland because Ireland had for very many years, as well as supplying priests and Sisters for the Irish Church, also supplied them to the English-speaking world. When I first arrived in Leeds the majority of priests were Irish. By the eighties this was no longer the case.

Numbers in the seminaries had begun to fall year on year. By the late eighties to the mid-nineties most of the Irish seminaries had been forced to close, or revert to offering secondary education or other services.

Part of the decline was undoubtedly caused by the scandal

of abuse. This first reared its monstrous head in Newfoundland in the late seventies. It soon began to emerge that it was a world-wide catastrophe. It emerged in Ireland in the mid-eighties. John Calnan, the prefect in junior house during my first year at Carlow College, spent several terms in prison for sexually assaulting young children. Some of the assaults occurred while the children were making their First Confession.

Most ordinary Catholics could handle the idea of a rotten apple in the barrel. What they could not accept was the failure of the Hierarchy to face up to and take full responsibility for the catastrophe. This issue remains unresolved, in the Catholic church worldwide, and in other church institutions, as well as many secular organisations involving minors.

A CHANGE OF STATUS FOR CARLOW COLLEGE, 1994

From 1793 Carlow College offered education to ecclesiastical and lay students. In 1892 it became exclusively a seminary. Under the leadership of Fr John McDonald, President 1986–1994, the transition from seminary back to being a lay college began to occur when lay students were invited to attend classes alongside seminarians.

Fr Caoimhín Ó Néill, President 1994–2015, masterminded the full transition from being a seminary to being an exclusively lay college. The last ordinations took place at Carlow College in 1994, two hundred and one years after the first students were enrolled. In 1995, the College was accepted into the Free Fees Initiative which meant that lay students had their fees paid by the state.

It was these students and their lecturers that I served as poet-in-residence. They studied and took degrees in theology, the humanities, and social care. Of these students the majority came straight from secondary schools in the surrounding towns of Leinster. A significant minority were mature students who had taken the opportunity to pursue third level education now that their children were old enough, or just because it was available to them.

I was particularly inspired by the dedication and resolve of these students: Doris from Wexford, who after participating in my weekly workshop signed up for the creative writing programme for the following year; Marie from Tullow, who had raised her kids and now wanted to pursue third level education for herself; or Ned from Abbeyleix who cycled the twenty two miles to Carlow and back each day come hail, rain or shine. I first met him in the gent's toilet drying his tracksuit, using both hand dryers simultaneously. He had developed this to a fine art. It had poured out of the heavens that morning and he kept a dry tracksuit in his locker for such occasions. He needed the wet one to be dry before he took the journey back home that evening.

Since 1995, Carlow College has functioned as a regional college offering degrees in the humanities and social sciences to people of the Irish midlands and beyond.

Poet-in-Residence
(September–December 2017)

Fifty four years almost to the day I first entered Carlow College, I was invited back by the current President Fr Conn Ó Maoldhomhnaigh to be poet-in-residence for the autumn semester. He had read a collection of poems I had written called *The Healing Station*. It was the result of a three-month writing residency at a unit for stroke and dementia patients at The Meath and Adelaide Hospital in Tallaght. *The Healing Station* featured poems (such as the following) inspired by patients healing from strokes or by members of the health-care team helping them.

Monica

'Would you like a cup of tea,' is always her first remark.
It's a long time since she's revelled in lavishing hospitality:
the family parties, big dinners, birthdays. Stuffed pork steak
was a speciality. But that's all gone now, along with everything.
The fall was inevitable, everybody said. Out in the yard

at the back of the care home. She thought she was
collecting tinder to start the fire. They found her
lying in a heap, with her pelvis fractured.

Today her son has come to visit. He intends to take her out
but the rain has started, so they do the internal tour instead.
Down the long corridor to the entrance and the coffee shop,
turn left, past the stairs to the children's ward, to the Chapel.

Lunchtime Mass is starting. She remembers the responses:
Lord have mercy. Christ have mercy. Lord have mercy.
After Communion she falls asleep. When she wakes
her son wheels her over to the healing stations.

He shows her the one with the woman who had an issue
of blood that had bothered her for twelve years. As Jesus
walks through the jostling crowd she touches the fringe
of his cloak, and he feels the power go out from him.

He's looking over his left shoulder to see who touched him.
The woman, barefoot, is down on one knee in the wet street.
Monica's eyes are filled with tears. 'You're a lovely man,'
she says to her son. 'Would you like a cup of tea.'

Fr Conn wondered if I might consider doing a similar residency
at my Alma Mater.

I felt hugely honoured. I had loved Carlow College from
the day I entered it. That love had stayed with me throughout
my life. Now I was being offered the chance to go back and meet
my eighteen-year-old self, and all the selves I had become in the
intervening years.

It was a blessed time. I enjoyed the challenges of being in a
very different Carlow College, set alongside my own experiences

going back over half a century. I led creative writing workshops, took tutorials, and joined with local writers' groups. I also read voraciously.

I had little interest in the College history when I was there as a student. A young man's concerns are focussed on the present and the future. When I came across a biography in the O'Keefe Library, *Life and Letters of Archpriest John Joseph Therry, Founder of the Catholic Church in Australia* by Rev. Eris M. O'Brien, published in 1922, I became engrossed in the character and the courage of John Therry.

I also read works by John England, Famine poet Richard Dalton Williams, John O'Leary, James Finton Lawlor, and other famous alumni. But Therry was the man who took my breath away. I was moved again and again by his indomitable spirit. The way he spoke truth to the powerful, and compassion to the powerless. I have used the letters verbatim, changing only line breaks and verse breaks to turn them into found poems.

Half way into the Residency I casually called into the George Bernard Shaw Theatre and the National Centre for Contemporary Art, situated about twenty yards from the College.

I discovered that *An Triail* by Máiréad Ní Ghráda was being performed the next day for Leaving Certificate students. There was one vacant seat. The play's subject matter, almost unmentionable in 1966, is now part of the national conversation.

The production was much finer than ours, but the synchronicity was not lost on me. It seemed to bring my time as a student and my time as poet-in-residence together in an unexpected and unifying way.

During the course of the residency I gave two public readings, one at the end of the first month, the second a few days before the end of the semester. I read some of the poems included here as 'work in progress', which of course they still are. The ones I include below specifically reflect on my time at the residency, though they naturally also include memories of my time as a student.

Passports

'Can I see your passports,' I joke, as they line up
To register. The four young women join in easy banter.
'We haven't brought them,' they tell me, as they stand
On the threshold. As I did in 1963.

Later, in the Cathedral where I was ordained
A surge of emotion rises. A lifetime ago.
Fragments of memory flicker onto my radar,
Things I did, and did not do well.

A sheltered eighteen year old come to study for the collar.
There were no young women walking these corridors then,
Just two hundred male students, us new arrivals wearing
Borrowed cassocks while our own were tailored.

We'd wear them for six years. These women
The knees of their jeans split in the current fashion
Fuse me to who I was. Meeting my history backwards
I surrender to the moment, embrace my younger self.

Moriarty Hall

Patrick Moriarty, 1805–7. Carlow College, 1817–22.
Founder of Villanova University, 1842. President, 1851–55.

This used to be the billiard room,
Though I was never a billiards man myself.
Acki was the king of the billiard table in our time,
He could score canons or pot the red from every angle.

Villanova was where Ronnie Delaney went to study
And win his gold medal at Melbourne Olympics in '56.
I was eleven. Delaney was my hero, my secret friend.
We trained together, running around the corn field.

We were evenly matched. He'd always let me win.
I never took the next step up. It wasn't in me.
I could run fast in my head but couldn't pass it
To my legs. I was no better than I was at billiards.

Years later I read something Delaney said:
'I wasn't a graceful runner, but I had these
Extraordinary legs, and when I ran to my best
I was like poetry. In fact I thought I was poetry.'

Thank you Patrick Moriarty for founding Villanova.
(And thanks to Jumbo Elliot who coached Delaney.)
I'm pleased to see this lecture hall dedicated to you.
Billiards doesn't come near what happens in it now.

Theology

This used to be the junior chapel, the altar
There at the front where the smart-board is,
Long wooden seats with the kneelers attached
Replaced by these blue chairs with adjustable shelves.

We gathered here for meditation each morning at 7am.
I hadn't much idea what meditation was. They said
It was prayer, but not recited prayers. All I knew
Was the half hour seemed to go on and on.

Barry Hall they call it now, the Freshers do theology here.
They're the same age we were, with the same uncertainties.
As they wait for the lecturer they consult their iPhones and chat.
It's something to do, it beats putting your hands in your pockets

And taking them out again. There were no iPhones then.
Some students had Crystal sets, though they weren't allowed.
An earpiece with two wires, attach one to the bed frame, earth the other
And, Radio Eireann. You could tell who had them: fellows who knew

The scores as we lined up for Vespers on Sunday night.
The lecturer, low key, sets up the equipment, introduces the class.
He shows us a video clip: Traditional, from *Fiddler on the Roof*.
We split into groups, discuss the layered meaning of the word.

After the break he slips in another word. Conventional.
Compare and contrast! We're being led deeper.
Back then theology taught us what to think.
Now it is teaching us how to think.

Custody of the Eyes

Custody of the eyes was to be considered whenever there were
Women about, which wasn't very often, but when the kitchen
Was temporarily short-staffed, Kate Carney, elderly matron
And catering manager for years, ruling with an iron hand,
Sequestered the First Divines to temporarily fill the gap.

John Francis Meagher, who was planning to leave shortly
Not only failed in regard to the above, but was also seen
More than once, exchanging nods and winks, as well as
Other inappropriate shenanigans involving a girl
From the kitchen, the handsomest there by far.

James Graham called a class meeting to discuss the crisis.
John Francis will have to be reported to the Dean, he says,
His conscience demands no less. Tommy Groome agrees.
Conscience, he says, is the bottom line. Moral Professor
Fr Larry Ryan in his lectures has been very clear on this.

Tommy, who will become a Professor himself, continues:
'If James Graham has an issue of conscience he is bound
To follow it, at whatever cost. However, a can of worms
Opens up here, because I too, though unaware of it
Until now, am also troubled by my conscience.

I have observed you James – and so have we all –
Repeatedly in cahoots, in a corner with Kate Carney.
I will now have to consider carefully how to proceed.'
James Graham's troubled conscience is eased at once.

The Handball Alley

I order Mushroom Risotto from the Specials, choosing it over
Beef Bourguignon, I'm wondering if I made the wrong call.
Donagh Carey's fine painting, inspired by Skellig Michael,
Observes me looking at it out of the corner of its eye.

Lennon Restaurant, part of Carlow Visual, with art exhibitions
Including the current instalment by Pat Collins called *Twilight*,
And the George Bernard Shaw Theatre, after the great man
Who had historic connections with the town.

Most of the evening diners haven't arrived yet. There's time
And space to meditate. This is where the handball alley was.
I had even less proficiency at handball than I had at other sports.
I was a bottom liner, which meant my partner would be top line.

I drew Frank Hession from Athenry, All Ireland Champion.
I couldn't fail. 'Put your arse against the wall,' he said to me
The first time we played, 'and don't move until I tell you.'
I served when it was my turn, otherwise I did exactly that.

Opponents tried to get me to get in the way but it didn't work.
We won without breaking sweat. The cups were of equal size,
Mine went on the dresser when I got home. People admired it
When they walked in. 'Mickey won it,' my father would say,

'For handball.' It is still in the house more than fifty years on.
The handball alley is long gone. Frank Hession left at the end
Of that first year, I wonder what became of him then?
I should have ordered the Beef Bourguignon.

Another Country

'What country are you from?' I ask.
'Ireland,' she says. I walked into that!
'What country are your parents from?' I say,
Trying to cover my tracks. 'Nigeria,' she tells me.

'Have you ever been there?' 'No,' she says.
'Maybe you'll get to visit someday,' I offer.
'Maybe you'll take your grandchildren there.'
'Maybe,' she smiles. I'm back on an even keel.

There were no students from Africa in our time.
'Go teach all nations' was a College motto.
We were going to save the world. There was
No such thing as Reverse Mission.

The nearest we had to dark skin was
A few lads from the west of Ireland who
Might have had Spanish blood, from the Armada.
Johnny Muggivan from Clare, he always had a tan.

So here is this fourth-year student, with a smile
To light up the Liffey. A Carlovian like myself.
I wonder if she is Igbo. The Biafran war raged
Back then, her parents would have been children,

Like the ones we saw nightly on our screens,
Being starved into submission. They were top
Of our sympathy list, fighting for independence.
They were in our prayers, and they were Catholic.

Later I grew to love the novels of Chinua Achebe,
Things Fall Apart, inspired by his love for Yeats.
Things come together now. The canvas broadens.
There are connections. I learn from my mistakes.

INTO THE FUTURE

With the Lord a day is like a thousand years,
and a thousand years are like a day.

2 Peter 3:8

The history of Carlow College, stretching over three hundred years from the birth of its founder James Keefe to the present, invites us to take the long-term view. The future of Carlow College is as important as its past.

The changes that take place within a culture or in a country, or indeed the broader changes that take place across the globe, are best looked at in the context of history.

Circumstances in Ireland at the beginning of the eighteenth century were very different to the circumstances of today. Yet each forms part of the overall story, as indeed does the future, however that future evolves.

The College crest above has 'Carlow College' at the top. Underneath it there is a tree, and underneath the tree a motif which reads: *'rescissa vegetior assurgit.'* 'That which has been cut back burgeons forth more abundantly.' Clearly a reference to the church emerging from the Penal era.

As a metaphor it retains all its power. May the College continueto flourish in the future, as it has throughout its long history.

Part Five
MY JOURNEY OF CONVERSION

INTIMATIONS

I arrived at St Malachy's parish in Halifax on 14th August 1969. It was a vast urban sprawl. There was a Sunday congregation of about 1500. A significant minority were unemployed, poor, or living on their wits. A big part of a curate's job was door-to-door visiting. I did this faithfully. There was a youth club which had known better times. I felt it was my task to revive it but had no idea how. The Parish Priest was elderly, and although faithful to the changes of Vatican II was less enthusiastic about it than I was. He still prayed the breviary in Latin.

I was particularly dedicated to my weekly homily, wanting it to be as good as I could make it, while also carrying a high level of anxiety about it. I'd stay up on a Saturday night until the early hours, honing and polishing, then wake with it being the first thing on my mind. I got compliments which gave me encouragement, and when no compliments appeared to be forthcoming I became anxious. A parishioner remarked in conversation that my sermons 'were awright.' I was seriously underwhelmed. I found out later that, in Halifax, to say something 'was awright' was the highest compliment one could receive.

I continued this process of intense preparation for several years until I grew in confidence. At a low moment years later a trusted friend said: 'You are the best communicator in the diocese, and the Bishop knows that.' That affirmation gave me a great lift that stayed with me for a long time.

After four years I was moved to St Clare's in Bradford. The Parish Priest was of the old style.

Vatican II had had a mainly negative impact on him, and he was suspicious about the new curate who was likely to have new ideas. He had also heard snippets about me which had led him to conclude I was one of these 'young buckos'.

Our differences were perfectly summed up by looking at the clothes line on wash day. His old style long johns at one end. My briefs in the current fashion and range of colours at the other end. It was a difficult time. People were supportive and in sympathy with me. Years later I discovered he was likely to have suffered from long-term depression. He always expressed the negative view, and apart from a very small number of friends, was almost always critical of parishioners. After a four year stand-off he moved to a one-man parish.

During my eight years at St Clare's I was also chaplain to St Joseph's College, an all-girls grammar school on the other side of Bradford. I grew to love this work. I began to offer day and overnight retreats for the pupils. We took a small number of older pupils to Lourdes each year to help with the sick, and particularly with children and adults with special needs.

During summer holidays we took a bus load of sixth formers on a two to three week camping trip to mainland Europe. Our main focus was Taizé, a simple ecumenical monastery founded by Brother Roger, close to Cluny. On our way down we'd spend a night or two in Paris, then a long weekend at Taize, before heading for the Swiss Alps. Lauterbrunnen was our favourite destination. The sheer wonder of the three great peaks, the Eiger, the Jungfrau, and the Monch took our breath away. We climbed the steep slopes, counted the waterfalls, and allowed ourselves to be saturated with the beauty all around us. For me it awakened the first intimations of poetry. The images stayed with me. More than two decades later I wrote the poem below. The speaker in the poem is the apostle John.

Transfiguration

We climbed over the ridge tops, along the ledge
clinging to the cliff face until we found a cave.
The sky was luminous. There were small left-over
wisps of cloud, blood-streaked by the set sun; then
the darkening light folding us in blacknesses.

It was a goat-herd woke us. We were slumbering
out of our skins, in the pre-alluvial dawn
when we heard them skittering on loose shale
munching the scruff around the cave mouth.

Afterwards, before the sun came up, we saw
in the shadows of the rock-face, the face of Moses.
Over there, the forehead with the brow furrowed
and below, the eyes still closed. The cheeks a pale
red ochre, turning yellow with morning; and the beard
falling away where the waterfall fanned out.

Elijah was next to him. That's what Peter said:
'just as we'd seen him in our ancestors' eyes.'
All I saw was greenery, a few bushy outcrops,
they could have been mistaken for eyebrows.
At that moment James came round a corner.
He'd been picking wild cranberries.

And then, as the sun splintered over the rim
Your face, impossibly bright, transparent with memory.
Not a single thing was hidden, everything translucent
simple, holier than we could imagine.

And in the silence: the tenor voice of small streams,
the far-away bass of the waterfall,
a single bird-note, and among them
the word Beloved.

After eight years at St Clare's I heard a rumour that I was to be moved to Leeds, to a parish where the Parish Priest and house-keeper were both alcoholics. I confess to low tolerance for people with alcohol issues. I was horrified. Discreet enquiries confirmed that this was the plan. It was time to act.

I had inherited a missionary focus from my uncle. China of course was not an option. The Columban Fathers however had a mission in Peru to which our diocese contributed both financially and with personnel. With the permission of my Bishop I volunteered to join the Columbans in Peru for six years.

Part of the preparation offered was a four-month programme called 'Faith and Mission'. Mixing with missionaries from different cultures and different countries was an enriching experience. I loved it. During the second half of the programme I was offered psychological tests to ascertain whether I was a suitable candidate, and how I might adjust to a different language and culture. When I met the psychologist for feedback I was blown out of the water.

Phrases like 'there is a lot of inferiority', 'serving on my strengths while trying to hide my weaknesses' and 'paying a heavy price in terms of anxiety' stay with me to this day. He finished by saying: 'You are not Superman, and you don't have to be.'

The psychologist asked me to question the wisdom of going ahead. I struggled with this for a couple of weeks. The most important factor was that I knew he had hit every single nail on the head.

I knew he had spoken the truth about who I was at that point.

He suggested that returning to Leeds, where I was well known and established and where my gifts were appreciated, would be a better base for going deeper. He gave me the addresses of a couple of psychologists I could work with for an extended period. And this was what I did. The Bishop was supportive, though he figured I was putting a brave face on something. Later, speaking to a Columban friend of mine, he asked him: 'Why was my man turned down?'

I spent the next two years seeing a priest, who was also a therapist, weekly. I wasn't sure exactly what was going on, but I knew it was helping me. One evening after my session, I went for a walk that took me past the presbytery garden, and imagined seeing an image of myself holding the globe of the world on my shoulders, just like that Charles Atlas image that was popular at the time. On my way back later, the image had changed. It was now a helium balloon that was tethered to a string, happily swaying in the breeze.

Not being Superman, and not having to be, was the insight on offer. Sometimes therapy was a hard road to travel. Getting in touch with feelings that had remained buried for years was a struggle. But gradually I had a sense of my rib cage expanding, and there was more of me that wanted to breathe the free air. It was the beginning of a change in my life where the focus became more on the inner than on the outer.

At this time I was working part time as administrator at St Mary's Selby, as well as being on the Youth Retreat Team at Woodhall, the Diocesan Pastoral Centre. The team leader was my friend Donal Lucey, ordained in Carlow in 1968. We had worked together previously, on school retreats, and on the summer camping trips to Taizé and Switzerland. Donal had leadership skills and was a good organiser. I had creative gifts for working with young people. Sr. Marie Gallagher was the third member of the team. She brought musical gifts.

I developed some of Donal's leadership and organisational skills, and he learned from my creativity and over time became an excellent communicator. Even if I say so myself we were a formidable team.

I became a Parish Priest for the first time in 1985. St Mary's, Bradford. It was the mother church of Bradford but most of the parishioners had now moved out to the suburbs. In June of my second year I received a phone call from a good friend, Bernard Bickers. He asked if he could come and speak to me about the possibility of becoming Spiritual Director/Counsellor at Ushaw College, the Major Seminary in Durham where he was Vice President.

I had been considering seeking training as a counsellor and there seemed some synchronicity about this phone call. After speaking with him I decided I would say yes, provided I could have proper personal and professional training. My Columban friend Eamonn O'Brien recommended a programme in Chicago run by Jesuit Paul Robb called 'The Institute for Spiritual Leadership'. I contacted them at once to enquire what was involved and how it worked.

They had a vacancy for the programme beginning in September. They sent me their materials and an application form. It was clear that a significant amount of affective self-knowledge was a requirement. I was accepted onto the programme and headed off to Chicago in early September 1987. It changed my life.

I shared a flat with Ben who worked as a missionary in Papua New Guinea, and Gill who had lived through the horrors of Rwanda. We shared cooking duties and other tasks, and went each day to Faber House for classes. Paul Robb was a genius of the Spiritual Journey, or as he called it: 'The Journey of Conversion'. This had been finely honed over many years and included many insights from the mystics, in particular St Ignatius of Loyola, St John of the Cross, and St Teresa of Avila. It also included insights from Transpersonal Psychology.

An hour-long lecture from Paul each morning was followed by classes that mainly involved experiential learning, Practicum in Spiritual Direction, Contemplative Attitude, Dream-work. There were process groups where we learned to explore our range of feelings and emotions.

Each participant had a two-hour session with their Spiritual Director each week. All of these different activities gradually took us deeper into our spiritual and affective selves. As we approached the Christmas break my first tears began to fall. The process continued to deepen in the second semester.

During the month of February my childhood anxieties begin to return. I'm fearful of being left out of things, being abandoned in some way by those on the programme with whom I have made deep friendships, looking for the attention of staff members, being increasingly dependent and needy. I am also touching into pockets of deep grief, which come to a head on 11th March 1988, the thirty eighth anniversary of my brother's death.

I'm having my weekly session with Anne, my spiritual director. I tell her I am dying with anxiety. She says, 'I can see that.' Suddenly something breaks within me and I hear these deep sobs coming up from the pit of my stomach. Anne invites me to lie on the floor and puts a blanket over me, and for two hours my whole body is engulfed by wave after wave of grief and sobbing. It's as if my whole body is releasing megawatts of static electricity. I am at once a forty two year old man and a four year old child. All the grief that had lain dormant for all these years has broken through the surface. It is an extraordinary experience. As I leave, Anne suggests I go to my flat, have a cup of tea followed by a quiet walk in the nearby park. 'Let yourself know the enormity of what has happened.'

Already I can feel my body is different. I feel lighter. I am seeing things with a clarity I have never seen before, as if with the eyes of a four year old in a forty two year old body. A couple of things are becoming clear to me. I was, and have always been a loved person. God is not a distant figure or a judge, but a lover who has loved me from the beginning. Jesus of Nazareth, as well as being the Son of God, is my brother. I too am a beloved son of God.

I also know that I will write poetry, even though I know little about the technical skills necessary. Those are things I can learn.

Over the next two weeks and over the Easter break there are several smaller episodes of what happened on 11th March. Gradually I notice a new freedom in my body. A more upright and loosened posture when I walk, and an evolving clarity in my eyes and face when I look in the mirror. I spend the rest of that semester growing into the space that has opened up within me, as indeed I have continued to do over the last thirty years.

Thirty years on I am still astounded at the miracle of healing that has taken place within me. Gone is the young, talented but needy person of my earlier years. Gone is the focus on mere externals. Inner life is what matters. The God of my life and how God is present in all of life.

I became less interested in what people might think, and more interested in living a life of integrity as deeply as I could. This was a gift that was offered to me, that I was able to share with others in retreats and workshops and in individual spiritual direction.

The Gift

And love, she said, was not
waiting for what had been expected
but more like listening to the river
that ran beneath your skin
was not the silver birch
spine stiff with anticipation
but more like the shiver of its leaves
upturned in the mid-morning wind.

And love, she said, was not
the breaking of some stone ghost
but more like the sound of water ebbing.
It came, she said, like a slow tide.

It crept across the shadows of trees
through the open skylight
into the bedroom of the boy
while his memory lay sleeping.

It came, she said
touching the space between his eyebrows,
fixing in his dark dreams
the broken axle to the wheel.

I began my six-year stint as spiritual director at Ushaw College in September 1988, which was later extended to eight years. They were blessed years. Not all of the students were comfortable with where I was coming from. Some were looking for easy pieties, whereas I was interested in something much deeper. Years later, some who were students at that time said to me: 'I didn't understand much of what you did with us at Ushaw, but I do now.'

I also discovered that I loved to teach. This was one area I had anxieties about, as when I was at Carlow College I felt I never got the hang of it.

During those years I began to write poetry. I also went incognito to poetry readings in Durham and Newcastle-upon- Tyne. I wanted to see how seasoned practitioners did it, hoping I would learn something. As indeed I did.

One night, a poet called Peter Armstrong read a poem about an old university mate whom he heard had become a priest. I knew this priest. He was from my diocese. When I next met Peter I mentioned the poem. We ended up in a nearby hostelry with several of his poet friends.

Peter asked if I wrote poetry and I confessed that I was a closet poet. He told me about this monthly workshop where he and some other poets met. Each one brought a poem which was read and then discussed by the group. He asked if I'd like to come along. And so it was that my apprenticeship to the craft of poetry began.

A couple of years later I was invited to join the Northern Workshop run by the poet and critic Sean O'Brien. This was a big shift in gear. I came each month with my latest poem. Poems were read then critiqued for twenty minutes while the reader had to remain silent. It was for the individual poet to accept or reject whatever comments were made.

I found it a challenging but hugely educational experience. I was amazed at the level of attention paid to my poems. I returned home after each session determined to absorb the insights offered, and returned the following month with a more complete poem.

By the spring of 1995 I was coming up to the last year of my contract at Ushaw College. I began to consider asking my Bishop for a three-month sabbatical. In early June I had my first poem accepted for publication. The following day I was diagnosed with colon cancer.

I drove out to the moors outside Durham, sat on the heather and wept. 'I'm just coming up to my fiftieth birthday. I don't want to die now.' This was my prayer.

The following Monday I had surgery, which was successful, and after spending the summer convalescing I was back at Ushaw for the first day of the new term. Thinking again about asking for sabbatical leave before I returned to parish work in Leeds, I thought, you only get the one chance. I wanted my poet self to develop and have a life of its own.

I wrote to my Bishop, David Constant, asking if I could take a sabbatical for a full year, to explore the interfaces between creativity and spirituality. He replied: 'I have no idea what this means, but it sounds like you and I think you should do it.'

I wrote to a number of Creative Writing Faculties and Schools of Theology in the United States and Canada. I had a reply from the University of Alberta saying they would be delighted to help me in any way they could, including office space if I needed it.

So Edmonton, Alberta it was. I finished my eight years at Ushaw, and that September fetched up in Edmonton. I'd never been to Canada. I felt that if I crossed geographical boundaries, psychological and other boundaries would also give way. I rented a small flat on a quiet street in Edmonton, where I would spend the next ten months, reading, meditating, and hopefully writing poetry.

On my second day in Edmonton I visited a bookshop in the local mall. A young, tall woman approached me and asked if she could help. I said I was fine, just browsing. She replied: 'In the poetry section.' I asked if she was a poet and she answered: 'Sort of.' I explained how I happened to be in Edmonton. I was hoping to meet the author of the book I was browsing. She told me if I went to a certain café that Friday evening I would meet most of the people who were part of the poetry scene in the city.

I went along as suggested and among others met a poet called Bert Almon, who ran the postgraduate creative writing programme. He invited me to join his Friday seminars as an extern. I would deliver a poem each week, pick up a poem from each of the other participants, read mine and be ready to discuss the others at the Friday seminar. As an extern, my poems would not be graded for exams.

He also told me the woman I met at the bookshop was the best young poet he had taught in years. Her name was Shawna Lemay, poet, essayist and novelist, and wife of the still life artist Rob Lemay. She has since published nine books, among them award winners and best sellers.

And so my year at Edmonton could not have got off to a better start. The weekly seminar provided a focus and a target for my writing and meditating. My reading list was made up of Canadian writers whom I was not familiar with. I was familiar with Leonard Cohen, but as a singer. I didn't know he had started out as a poet.

I also spent lots of time reading the early books of the Old Testament and became engrossed in the character of Moses. I wrote a long prose poem imagining what being Moses was like. I called it 'Not Written on Stone.'

That winter the temperature dropped to minus 45°C. Being so cold outside was a great incentive to stay in and read and write. I made a lot of friends in Edmonton, became mildly well known, including a brief appearance on local TV and having my poems broadcast on BBC Canada. I returned to England in July 1997 with a body of work.

While on holiday in Ireland in August of that summer I read about a competition called The Patrick Kavanagh Award, open to poets who had not yet published a full manuscript. I put together the required number of poems, sent off the pamphlet and thought no more about it. In early November I received a phone call telling me I had been named the winner. You could have knocked me over with a feather. I had loved Kavanagh's poems all my life because of their spiritual and mystical dimensions. And here I was, heading off to Inniskeen to receive the Patrick Kavanagh Award. The thrill of it has stayed with me ever since.

The title of the pamphlet was *Birds' Nests and Other Poems*. It later became my first published collection. The poem below comes from that collection and is as good a place to end as any.

In Memoriam

Let's say the year is twenty-one-sixteen.
The headstone says I died in twenty-thirty-six.
Though I've been dead these eighty years
I'm pleased to see I lived to ninety one.

The graveyard perched
above an S of sea where boats can rest
along a lonely curve of shore
where tourists no longer come.

Beneath my name: the dates of birth and death,
some long-forgotten lines I haven't written yet.
Beside my grave a grass-grown gravel path
unused except by fishermen at night.

I see a woman pushing back the grass.
She's twenty-five or so.
Researching for her PhD, her subject:
Forgotten Irish Poets.
She found some poems of mine on micro-disk
buried in the archives of a library
in Edmonton Alberta, where
I was almost famous once.

She stands among small raindrops
as I once stood
in the graveyard at Drumcliff.
She weeps as I wept over Yeats.
A strand of hair clings to her face.
A briar sways in unnoticed wind.
Far below the waves say hush.
Close by a blackbird sings.